Contents

* against a module denotes it as a module assessed only by terminal examination.

How to use this book

The revision guide contains the 12 modules that form the AQA Modular Science scheme. They cover the Higher Tier of the syllabus.

You will need to learn and understand these six modules for module tests during the course:

AT2	AT3	AT4
Humans as organisms	*Metals*	*Energy*
Maintenance of life	*Earth materials*	*Electricity*

You will need to learn and understand these six modules for the terminal exam:

AT2	AT3	AT4
Environment	*Patterns of chemical change*	*Forces*
Inheritance and selection	*Structures and bonding*	*Waves and radiation*

You will also have to revise certain areas of the first group of six modules above for the terminal exam. These are very clearly marked by an orange tint, as shown here.

As you approach a module test or the terminal exam in your course, you can organise your work like this.

Work through the module or modules you need. Pace yourself – do one double page spread at a time and look back at the notes you have made in class on this topic.

Try the questions at the end of every double page spread to check that you really understand the topic.

Check your answers under *Answers to end of spread questions* (page 143). Go back over anything you find difficult.

Do the test style questions at the end of each module. These are in the same style as the questions you will have to do in the real end of module test or terminal exam, so they are very good practice.

Check your answers against the *Answers to module tests and terminal exam questions* (page 130). In terminal exam style questions take care to cover all the points needed to get full marks. Go back over areas you find difficult.

When you are revising for the terminal exams you will also need to revise the material marked with an orange tint in the other six modules. Revise these alongside modules in the same AT. For example, as you work through *Structures and bonding* or *Patterns of chemical change* in AT3 it would be a good idea to revise the terminal exam material in *Metals* or *Earth materials* at the same time.

The words in **bold** are all key words you need to know. A useful revision idea would be to build up your own glossary of these as you work through the book. For quick reference to a word or topic use the *Index*, which starts on page 152.

Life processes and living things

Humans as organisms

Maintenance of life

Environment

Inheritance and selection

Cells

Cells make up animals and plants. Most animal cells have:

- a nucleus that controls what the cell does
- a cell membrane that controls the passage of substances in and out of the cell
- enzymes that control these chemical reactions
- mitochondria – small structures in the cytoplasm where energy is released through respiration.
- cytoplasm in which the chemical reactions take place.

The structures of some cells are adapted or **specialised** to help them perform particular jobs in your body.

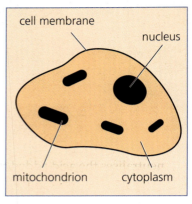

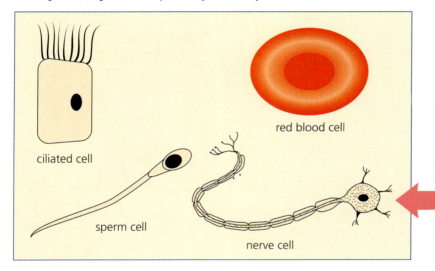

red blood cell

ciliated cell

sperm cell

nerve cell

Cells grouped together make up **tissues**, and different tissues make up **organs**. A group of organs forms an **organ system**. Specialised cells, tissues, organs and systems have different **functions** in the body.

Eating and digestion

The human digestive system ('the gut') turns food we eat into a form that can be used by the body cells.

Much of the food we eat is insoluble (for example, starches, proteins and fats). This food needs to be digested in the gut so that the large insoluble lumps are broken down into small soluble molecules that can be absorbed into and carried by the blood. This breakdown of larger molecules into smaller ones is speeded up (catalysed) by **enzymes**.

The food you eat includes **carbohydrates** and **fats** for energy, and **proteins** for growth and replacing damaged cells.

Organ	Enzyme(s) produced	Action
salivary gland	amylase	starch to sugar
stomach	protease	protein to amino acids
small intestine	amylase	starch to sugar
	protease	protein to amino acids
	lipase	fats to fatty acids and glycerol

The soluble molecules are absorbed into the blood through the wall of the small intestine. Some food cannot be digested and this passes into the large intestine. Here, most of the water is absorbed from it. The remainder passes out of the body as faeces. Most of the faeces is indigestible food and it leaves the body by the anus.

Bile is produced in the liver and stored in the gall bladder. It has two functions.

■ As food enters the small intestine bile neutralises the acid added to it in the stomach. It makes conditions in the small intestine alkaline, allowing the enzymes to work there more effectively.

■ It breaks down large fat globules into smaller ones, resulting in a larger surface area for enzymes to work on. This is known as emulsification.

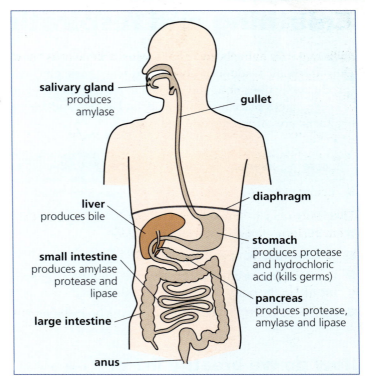

The human digestive system

Diffusion

The soluble molecules in the small intestine pass into our bloodstream by diffusion. This is the movement of particles from a region of high concentration to one of lower concentration. The blood circulating around the small intestine while a meal is being digested has a lower concentration of simple sugars, amino acids, mineral ions and water than the mixture flowing through the small intestine. The molecules therefore diffuse out through the walls of the small intestine.

This diffusion is helped by the structure of the small intestine walls. They are covered by millions of small, finger-like projections called **villi** (*singular* villus) These help the food diffuse through the wall because they:

■ slow down the passage of food through the small intestine

■ provide a very large surface area for the absorption to take place.

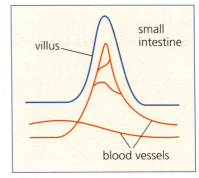

Villus

Questions

1 Make a table showing where the different enzymes are made and what they do.

2 The enzymes in the small intestine need alkaline conditions to work in. What conditions do the stomach enzymes need to work in?

3 Explain why emulsifying fat droplets helps the lipase enzymes to work on them.

Breathing and respiration

All living cells in the body respire, usually by **aerobic respiration**. During aerobic respiration chemical reactions use glucose (produced by digestion) and oxygen to release energy. This release of energy takes place in **mitochondria**. The by-products (waste products) are carbon dioxide and water.

> **glucose + oxygen → carbon dioxide + water + energy**

This energy is used:

- ■ to allow body muscles to contract
- ■ to keep body temperature constant
- ■ to build large useful substances from the small digested ones, for use in the body
- ■ for **active transport** of materials across boundaries.

Active transport
This is the movement of certain particles from a dilute solution to a more concentrated one. This is opposite to the way substances normally diffuse, so energy is needed to make it happen. It is called active transport because substances have to be 'pushed' across cell boundaries against the normal flow.

How do we breathe in?

When we breathe in:

- ■ the muscles between the ribs contract so that the ribs move up and out
- ■ at the same time the muscles of the diaphragm contract and it flattens
- ■ the space inside the thorax (chest) increases and the lungs get larger
- ■ this causes a decrease in air pressure in the lungs
- ■ atmospheric pressure outside is higher, so air rushes in.

... and to breathe out, the process happens in reverse.

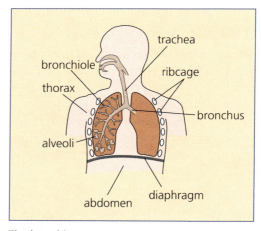

The breathing system

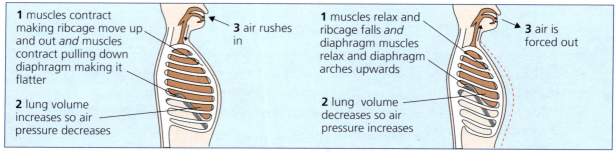

Breathing in

... and breathing out

How are gases exchanged with the blood?

The oxygen we breathe in diffuses into the air sacs (**alveoli**) of the lungs. It then diffuses through the walls of the alveoli into the surrounding blood capillaries. Carbon dioxide diffuses from the blood in the capillaries into the air sacs.

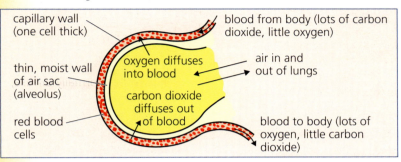

Gas exchange inside the lungs

The lungs have features that make them efficient at exchanging these gases:

- a very large, moist surface area
- a very good capillary blood supply.

> **Diffusion**
> This is the movement of a gas, or a substance in solution, from an area of high concentration to one of low concentration. The greater the difference in concentration, the greater the rate of diffusion. No energy is required.

Not enough oxygen?

Sometimes, for example when you are running fast, you cannot get enough oxygen into your lungs for the needs of your muscles.

Anaerobic respiration then takes over. This is respiration without using oxygen. Body cells break down glucose incompletely, into lactic acid, to produce just enough energy for them to work. Lactic acid causes muscle fatigue, so the body can't respire anaerobically for very long.

When you stop running you still breathe hard. This is because you need the oxygen to break down the lactic acid, releasing carbon dioxide and water. You have built up an **oxygen debt**, which has to be repaid by oxidising the lactic acid.

Questions

1. How does the body get the glucose and oxygen needed for respiration?
2. What happens to the carbon dioxide produced by cells during respiration?
3. Explain why the large surface area provided by the alveoli helps the diffusion of gases.
4. Explain why oxygen diffuses into the blood around the lungs and carbon dioxide diffuses out of it.
5. Write a brief description of what happens to the ribs, diaphragm and lungs when you breathe out.
6. Why do you continue to breathe hard after you have finished running?

The circulatory system

This contains **blood**, which is made up of red cells, white cells and platelets carried in a fluid called plasma.

Plasma transports:

- carbon dioxide from all cells in the body's organs to the lungs
- digested food (mostly glucose) from the small intestine to organs
- urea from the liver to the kidneys.

The red cells transport:

- oxygen from the lungs to the cells (organs).

Parts of the blood

Red cells have no nucleus but lots of **haemoglobin**. As the blood passes the lungs the haemoglobin picks up the oxygen to form **oxy-haemoglobin**. The oxygen is released as the blood passes respiring cells.

White cells have a nucleus. They help defend the body against microorganisms (bacteria).

Platelets are small cell fragments. They don't have a nucleus and help to form clots (scabs over cuts).

Plasma is the liquid part of the blood.

The circulation system

There are two circulation systems:

- one to the lungs
- one to the rest of the body.

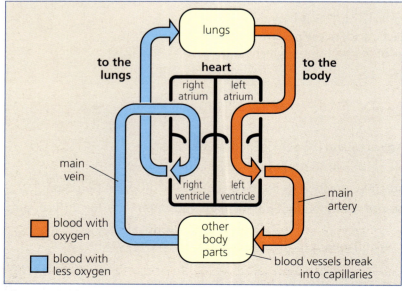

The two circulation systems

The blood enters the two atria of the heart. The muscles of the atria contract and force the blood into the ventricles. The muscles of the ventricles now contract and force the blood out of the heart. This happens on both sides of the heart at the same time.

The different blood vessels

Arteries take blood away from the heart under high pressure. They have thick, muscular, elastic walls so that they don't burst when the heart beats.

Veins bring blood back to the heart under low pressure. They have thinner walls and also have valves along their length to prevent backflow of blood. This is especially important when it is coming back from the feet!

Capillaries are very, very small. Their walls are only one cell thick to allow the exchange of substances with the cells. Oxygen diffuses from the red blood cells in the capillaries to the cells of the body. Carbon dioxide diffuses from these body cells into the blood. Glucose and other useful substances in the plasma diffuse out of the capillary to reach the cells.

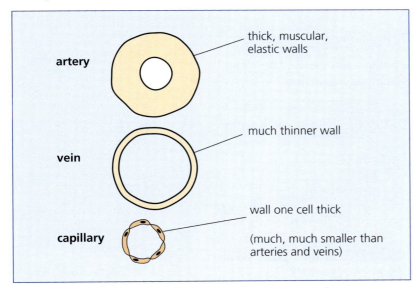

artery — thick, muscular, elastic walls

vein — much thinner wall

capillary — wall one cell thick (much, much smaller than arteries and veins)

Types of blood vessel

Questions

1   What is transported in the plasma?

2   How is the structure of a vein different to that of an artery?

3   What substances are exchanged between the capillaries and the body cells?

4   What are the functions of white cells, red cells and platelets?

5   Trace the journey of a red cell from entering the left atrium of the heart to its arrival at the right atrium.

Disease

What causes disease? One of the main causes is when
microorganisms such as certain **bacteria** and **viruses**, get into the
body. These cause a whole range of illnesses, from the common
cold to meningitis and AIDS.

Microorganisms

A bacterial cell has cytoplasm surrounded by a cell membrane. All
of this is surrounded by a cell wall. It has no nucleus.

Usually the genes that allow a cell to reproduce and make copies of
itself are in the nucleus. In bacteria the genes are in the cytoplasm.

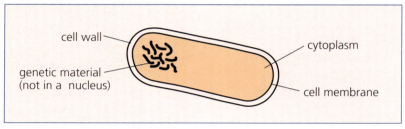

A bacterium

Viruses are much smaller than bacteria. They are very different to
cells. They have a protein coat surrounding a few genes. They can
only reproduce inside the living cells of other organisms.

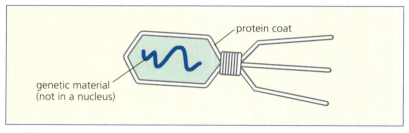

A virus

If large numbers of microorganisms (bacteria or viruses) enter your
body then you may catch a disease. The microorganisms can
reproduce very quickly inside your body so that there are soon
millions of them. They may produce **toxins** (poisons) that make
you feel ill.

If a virus reproduces inside one of your cells the cell will be damaged.

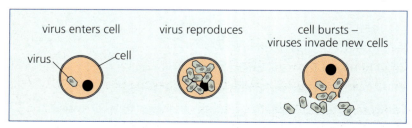

A virus reproducing

Defence against disease

The best defence is to stop the bugs getting in! Your body does this in several ways.

- Your skin acts as protection. If you have a cut microorganisms can get straight into your blood.
- Blood clots to form a scab. This seals cuts in the skin and stops microorganisms getting in.
- Air passages in your nose and lungs have a thick, sticky mucus on their surface inside to trap microorganisms. When you blow your nose or cough you are getting rid of these trapped microorganisms.
- Your stomach contains acid that can kill most microorganisms.

If the microorganisms get into your body then the white cells take action. They:

- ingest (eat) the microorganisms
- produce **antibodies** that help destroy particular microorganisms
- produce **antitoxins** to neutralise (get rid of) the poisons.

Once white cells have produced antibodies against a particular microorganism then the next time the microorganism enters your body they can produce the right antibodies more quickly. Your body is said to be **immune** to the microorganism.

Vaccination is when you are injected with a mild or dead form of an infecting microorganism. The white cells produce antibodies in response. If the infective microorganism enters your body in the future, then more antibodies are quickly produced to destroy it.

Disease and lifestyle

How do you come into contact with harmful microorganisms? There are two main ways.

- When ill people cough or sneeze they release a fine spray that contains microorganisms. If you breathe these in you risk catching the same illness.
- If you eat food prepared in unhygienic conditions or drink unclean water then you may become ill. Unclean water is often found when large numbers of people are crowded into one place without proper sewage treatment systems. Dirty water can carry cholera, which spreads very fast and is very dangerous.

People have known about infectious diseases for centuries, but it was only in the 1800s that they began to find out what caused them and how they spread.

Cholera was a new disease to hit Britain in the 1830s. Most doctors thought it was spread by touch or 'bad air'. A turning point came in 1854, when hundreds of Londoners died in a cholera epidemic. Dr John Snow thought the disease might be passed through water, so he recorded where each of the victims lived. By plotting this information on a local map he saw that they all got their water from a pump in Broad Street. He persuaded the authorities to have the pump handle removed, and quickly the epidemic began to subside.

Questions

1. How are viruses different from cells?
2. What are toxins and how does the body get rid of them?
3. If microorganisms do get into the body and disease results, what does the body do about it?
4. How are microorganisms prevented from getting into the body?
5. Sometimes in dense populations disease is able to spread very fast. Why is this?

Module test questions

1 These sentences are about the blood system.

Choose words from the list for each of the spaces 1–4 in the sentences.

white cells   platelets
plasma   red cells

Oxygen is carried by ____**1**____ in the bloodstream. The liquid part of the blood is called ____**2**____. Normally the skin keeps microorganisms out but if the skin is cut, ____**3**____ help to form blood clots. If microorganisms do get into the blood, then ____**4**____ help defend the body.

2 These sentences are about how we breathe in.

Choose words from the list for each of the spaces 1–4 in the sentences.

decreases   increases
flattens   contracts

When we breathe in the diaphragm ____**1**____ as the muscle ____**2**____. The space inside the thorax ____**3**____ and the pressure therefore ____**4**____.

3 This table is about digestion and parts of the gut. Match words from the list with each of the numbers 1–4 in the table.

large intestine   pancreas
liver   stomach

	Function of the part
1	produces protease and hydrochloric acid
2	produces bile
3	absorbs much of the water
4	produces protease, carbohydrase and lipase

4 Which **two** of the following statements are correct?

Bile is a liquid that:

   A breaks down fats to fatty acids and glycerol

   B neutralises stomach acid

   C breaks down fat droplets

   D is produced by the gall bladder

   E works in the large intestine

5 Which **two** of the following statements are correct?

Arteries are blood vessels that:

   A take blood away from the heart at high pressure

   B have valves along their length

   C have thin, muscular walls

   D have thick, elastic walls

   E return blood to the heart under low pressure

6 This is a diagram of the gut.

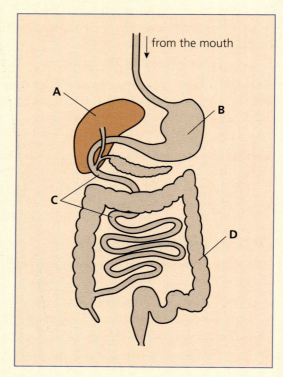

1. In which part is bile produced?

   A   B   C   D

2. In which part does most absorption of water take place?

   A   B   C   D

3. In which part are the products of digestion mainly absorbed?

   A   B   C   D

4. In which part does fat digestion take place?

   A   B   C   D

7 This is a diagram of the circulatory system.

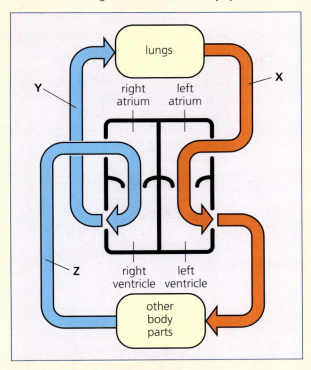

1. The blood vessel labelled X is:

   A an artery carrying oxygenated blood
   B a vein carrying oxygenated blood
   C an artery carrying deoxygenated blood
   D a vein carrying deoxygenated blood

2. The blood vessel labelled Y is:

   A an artery carrying oxygenated blood
   B a vein carrying oxygenated blood
   C an artery carrying deoxygenated blood
   D a vein carrying deoxygenated blood

3. The blood vessel labelled Z has the following features:

   A thick walls and no valves
   B elastic walls and no valves
   C valves and thin walls
   D muscular walls which are thin

4. In order to be efficient capillaries have:

   A valves
   B muscular walls
   C a large surface area
   D elastic tissue

8 These are diagrams of a bacterium and a virus.

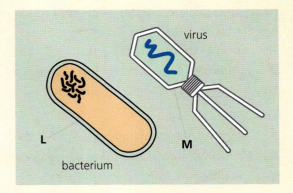

1. The part labelled L is:

   A a cell membrane
   B a protein coat
   C a nuclear membrane
   D a cell wall

2. The part labelled M is:

   A a cell wall
   B a protein coat
   C a cell membrane
   D the nuclear material

3. Which part of the blood helps to destroy microorganisms?

   A white cells
   B platelets
   C red cells
   D plasma

4. The function of antibodies is to:

   A attack microorganisms on their own
   B help the blood to clot
   C destroy poisons (toxins)
   D allow the white cells to attack certain microorganisms

Plant and animal cells

Like animals, plants are made up of cells. Plant and animal cells have the following parts:

- a **nucleus** controlling the cell
- **cytoplasm** where the chemical reactions take place
- a **cell membrane** allowing substances in and out.

Plant cells also have:

- a **cell wall**, which maintains a rigid shape
- **chlorophyll** for photosynthesis (in **chloroplasts**)
- a **vacuole** containing cell sap.

Some cells are specialised to do certain work. Groups of cells with the same structure and function are called **tissues**. In plants, xylem cells make up **xylem** tissue, which transports water. Different tissues make up an **organ** (for example, a leaf).

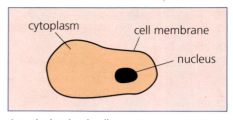

A typical animal cell

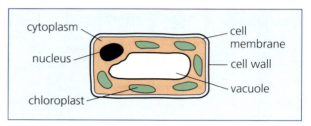

A typical plant cell

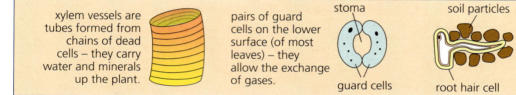

xylem vessels are tubes formed from chains of dead cells – they carry water and minerals up the plant.

pairs of guard cells on the lower surface (of most leaves) – they allow the exchange of gases.

these cells are able to take in water from the soil – they provide a large surface area.

How do plants make their food?

Plants make their food by **photosynthesis**. Light provides the energy for the process:

- green chlorophyll traps (absorbs) the light energy
- the energy is used to make glucose by combining carbon dioxide and water
- oxygen is released as a waste product.

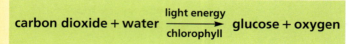

carbon dioxide + water $\xrightarrow[\text{chlorophyll}]{\text{light energy}}$ **glucose + oxygen**

The rate of photosynthesis can be limited by:

- low temperature
- shortage of carbon dioxide
- too little light.

If you were growing lots of plants in a greenhouse it might be an idea to heat it. This would work as long as there was enough carbon dioxide and light getting into the greenhouse. If either light or carbon dioxide was in short supply you would be wasting your money because the plants couldn't photosynthesise any faster, no matter how much you heat the greenhouse.

Carbon dioxide

Carbon dioxide enters the plant through holes in the surface of the leaves, called **stomata**. It moves into the leaf by diffusion. It diffuses from a higher concentration of carbon dioxide in the air to an area of lower concentration in the leaf. Inside the leaf it also moves to the cells by diffusion. The flattened shape and air spaces inside the leaf provide a large surface area for air to reach cells.

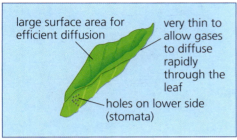

Structure of a leaf

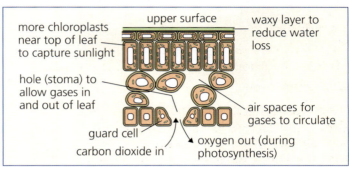

Section through a leaf

Respiration

The glucose produced during photosynthesis can be stored as insoluble starch or used to release energy in respiration.

This energy can be used to build smaller molecules (particles) into larger ones for growth. Energy is used to change:

- sugars (glucose) into **starch** for storage
- sugars into **cellulose** for cell walls
- sugars, nitrates and some other nutrients into amino acids, which are then built up into **proteins** for growth.
- sugars into lipids (fats and oils) for storage in seeds.

For healthy growth plants also need mineral ions taken from the soil through their roots:

- **nitrate** – makes proteins for growth
- **potassium** – helps the enzymes controlling photosynthesis and respiration
- **phosphate** – important in photosynthesis and respiration.

If a plant lacks some of these nutrients (ions) then the symptoms are shown in the table.

Nutrient lacking	Symptoms
nitrate	stunted growth with yellow, older leaves
phosphate	poor root growth and purple younger leaves
potassium	yellow leaves with some dead areas

Questions

1   Use a spider diagram to show all the parts a plant cell has that an animal cell does not have.
2   Why do lawns not need cutting in winter?
3   How does carbon dioxide get to the cells in a plant?
4   Give **three** uses for the sugars that plants produce.
5   A plant is not taking up enough phosphate. How could you tell by looking at it?
6   What is the equation for photosynthesis?

Transport in plants

Water

Plants take up water mostly through **root hair** cells on their roots. The root hairs provide a very large surface area for absorbing water.

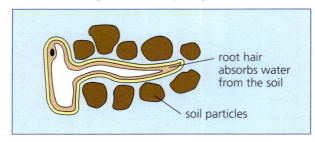

root hair absorbs water from the soil

soil particles

A root hair cell

Water is transported to all of the other cells in the plant. In flowering plants the **xylem** vessels transport water and minerals from the roots to the stem, leaves and other parts. **Phloem** vessels transport sugars from the leaves to all parts of the plant, but particularly to growing points and storage areas.

Osmosis

Water moves into the root hair cells by **osmosis**.

You can see from the diagram that there is a greater concentration of water molecules to the right of the cell membrane (the part that is only water). There is a lower concentration of water molecules in the sugar solution. There is therefore a **concentration gradient** between the two. Water molecules will move both ways in a random way. However, more will move from the water to the sugar solution than the other way. We say that there is a **nett movement** from the water to the sugar solution.

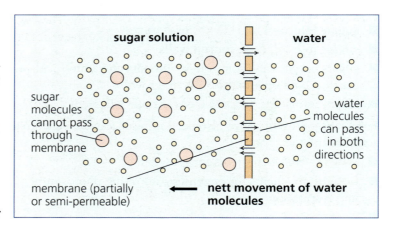

sugar solution   water

sugar molecules cannot pass through membrane

water molecules can pass in both directions

membrane (partially or semi-permeable)

nett movement of water molecules

Water helps to keep a plant upright. It enters cells and increases the pressure inside them. Cell walls can resist this pressure and so it keeps the cell rigid. This is known as cell **turgor** and helps support the plant. A small seedling cannot stand up on its own without enough water – it **wilts**. However, plants do not want to take up too much water so they store the sugar they produce as starch – starch is insoluble and has no effect on osmosis.

Keeping the water

Plants lose water by evaporation from the leaves (**transpiration**). Much of this takes place through the stomata. If a plant loses more water than it can take up, it will wilt.

More water transpires on hot, dry, windy days.

Plants can reduce water loss by:

- closing the stomata – this is done by changing the shape of the guard cells that surround each stoma
- having a waxy layer on the upper surface of their leaves that stops too much water escaping. Plants that live in hot, dry conditions have a thicker waxy layer.

Active transport

Sometimes substances have to be absorbed into cells against a concentration gradient. For example, roots take up nutrients such as phosphates, nitrates and potassium from the soil where they may be in a more dilute solution than in the roots themselves. The plant uses energy from respiration to move them across cell boundaries against the concentration gradient.

How do plants respond?

Plants are sensitive to light, moisture and gravity:

- their shoots grow towards light and against the force of gravity
- their roots grow towards moisture and in the direction of gravity.

These responses are caused by **hormones**. Plants produce hormones that can collect unevenly in different parts. They will therefore cause uneven growth rates, which make the shoot or the root of the plant bend in the right direction.

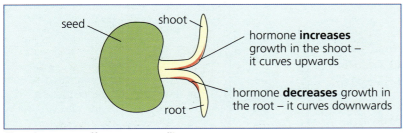

Plant hormone effects on a seedling

Plant hormones can be used to:

- help root cuttings to grow, so making large numbers of new plants quickly
- ripen fruit at the time the grower wants it to ripen
- kill weeds by making them grow so rapidly they die.

Questions

1 How are root hair cells adapted to maximise water uptake?

2 What is meant by the term 'osmosis'?

3 Use a spider diagram to show the different ways that humans use plant hormones. Put **plant hormones** at the centre of the diagram.

How do humans respond?

The nervous system makes it possible for your body to respond to changes in your surroundings (or **stimuli**). Cells called **receptors** can detect many different stimuli.

Receptors in	are sensitive to	which means
eye	light	you can see
ear	sound	you can hear
ear	changes in position	you can balance
tongue and nose	chemicals	you can taste and smell
skin	pressure and temperature	you can feel heat and different textures

Information from receptors passes along **neurones** (nerve cells) to the **central nervous system** (brain and spinal cord), which **coordinates** the response.

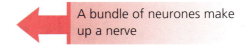

A bundle of neurones make up a nerve

Reflex actions ●

Responses that happen automatically and very quickly are called **reflex actions**.

This is a typical reflex action:

- ■ **Receptors** (for example, in the retina) send impulses (electrical charges) along a **sensory neurone** (for example, in the optic nerve) to the central nervous system.

- ■ At the junction with a **relay neurone** a chemical is released. The junction is called a **synapse**.

- ■ This chemical triggers an impulse through the relay neurone.

- ■ At the junction with the correct **motor neurone** a chemical is released again.

- ■ Impulses travel along the motor neurone to the muscle or gland, which will do something (the **effector**) in response to the impulse from the neurone.

- ■ The muscle will contract or the gland will produce a hormone or enzyme.

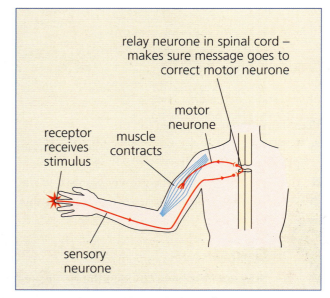

A reflex arc

stimulus → receptor → coordinator → effector → response
(central nervous system)

The eye • • • • • • • •

The diagram shows the structure of the eye.

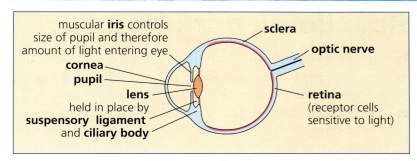

Cross-section through the human eye

When you look at an object:

■ light reflected from the object enters through the **cornea**

■ the cornea and **lens** focus this light on the **retina**

■ receptor cells in the retina send impulses to the brain along the **optic nerve**

■ the brain interprets the impulses (you 'see' the object) and coordinates the necessary response.

The shape of the lens can be changed to focus on near or distant objects, so:

■ with near objects the light rays have to be 'bent' more – the lens is quite thick

■ with distant objects the light rays need to be 'bent' less – the lens will be much thinner.

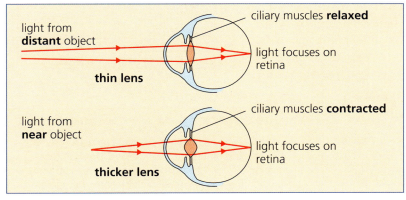

How the eye focuses

The response is automatic. You don't have to think, 'I must change the shape of my lens!' It is a reflex action.

Questions

1 You touch a hot kettle. You pull your hand out of the way. Describe the reflex arc that results when this happens.

2 How are impulses carried in the nervous system?

3 You were watching the television but then looked out of the window at a friend walking through the gate. The television picture and then your friend were both in focus. What happened in your eye to make this happen?

Regulating our internal environment

We produce waste and need to get rid of it. Our waste includes:

- **carbon dioxide** – produced during respiration, excreted through the lungs
- **urea** – produced in the liver by the breakdown of excess amino acids, removed by the kidneys in the urine, which is stored in the bladder.

Other internal conditions that need to be controlled include:

- **water content** of the body – water is lost from the lungs in breathing out and through the skin in sweating; excess water is lost in the urine
- the **ion content** of the body – ions are lost through sweating and in urine
- **temperature** – it is vital to maintain the temperature at which body enzymes work best; sweating helps to cool the body
- the level of **sugar** in the bloodstream.

Hormones coordinate much of what happens inside us. They are carried in the bloodstream and act on specific organs.

The kidneys

Blood arriving at the kidneys contains many useful substances (for example, glucose) as well as waste (some salts, urea and excess water). Tubules in the kidneys filter the blood and:

- reabsorb all the sugar
- reabsorb some dissolved salts (ions) needed by the body (by active transport if necessary)
- reabsorb the water needed by the body.

The filtered blood leaving the kidneys now contains only useful substances. The waste (urine) is drained from the kidneys by the ureter to the bladder.

How do the kidneys 'know' how much water to reabsorb? This is controlled by the pituitary gland in the brain.

main vein takes filtered blood from kidney

main artery takes blood to kidney

kidney filters the blood

ureter carries urine to bladder

The control of water in the body

Too little water in blood	Too much water in blood
pituitary gland produces more ADH (antidiuretic hormone), which causes the kidneys to reabsorb more water, making the urine more concentrated	pituitary gland produces less ADH, which causes the kidneys to absorb less water, making the urine less concentrated.

Body temperature

This is controlled by a **thermoregulatory centre** in the brain. Sensory cells (receptors) are sensitive to the temperature of the blood flowing through the brain. Receptor cells in the skin also send messages to the centre. Most important is the core body temperature. This is the temperature in the central part of your body that contains the main organs.

Core temperature too high	Core temperature too low
blood vessels supplying capillaries in the skin dilate, so that more blood flows near the skin's surface and more heat is lost	blood vessels supplying the skin's capillaries constrict
sweat glands release sweat, which uses the heat of the skin to evaporate, so cooling the body	muscles may 'shiver' – the respiration to provide the energy for this movement releases heat

Blood sugar level

The hormones **insulin** and **glucagon** control blood sugar levels. They are produced in the pancreas.

Diabetes is a disease in which someone's pancreas does not produce enough insulin. Because of this the blood sugar level can rise too high and cause death. Diabetes can be controlled by a careful diet and by injecting insulin into the blood.

Sugar level too high	Sugar level too low
pancreas releases insulin into the blood – this makes the liver convert excess sugar to insoluble glycogen, which is stored	pancreas releases glucagon into the blood – this makes the liver convert glycogen to glucose (sugar), which is released into the blood

How do drugs affect our bodies?

Solvents, alcohol, tobacco and other drugs can harm our bodies.

- Solvents affect behaviour and may cause damage to lungs, liver and brain.
- Tobacco smoke can cause lung cancer, other lung diseases, for example emphysema, and disease of the heart and blood vessels.
- Alcohol affects the nervous system by slowing down reactions. This can lead to lack of self control, unconsciousness and possibly coma. It may also affect the liver and brain.

Carbon monoxide (present in tobacco smoke) combines irreversibly with haemoglobin in red blood cells. This reduces how much oxygen the blood can carry. In pregnant women this can result in less oxygen getting to the baby and therefore a lower birth mass.

Up to about 1950 no-one realised the health risks of smoking. It was big business and highly fashionable. Gradually some scientists began to link smoking with lung disease, but it took many years for the public to accept this. Other things such as car exhaust fumes also cause lung disease. Lung cancer takes 10–20 years to develop – scientists could prove the link only by comparing the number of deaths among smokers with non-smokers, over several decades. When people did start to give up smoking, the number of deaths from lung cancer began to drop. Scientists have now found that chemicals in tar from cigarettes can cause cells to mutate (change), causing cancer.

Questions

1. After playing a game of basketball you look bright red. How would you explain this?
2. On a hot day you do not produce much urine. How would you explain this?
3. Which **two** organs do both solvents and alcohol affect?
4. A large number of people die from lung cancer every year. Which other system in the body does smoking badly affect?
5. How does alcohol affect the nervous system?

Module test questions

1 This table is about cells and the jobs the different parts have.

Match words from the list with each of the numbers 1–4 in the table.

nucleus　　**cytoplasm**
cell wall　　**choloroplast**

	Job
1	traps the Sun's energy for photosynthesis
2	controls the activities of a cell
3	maintains the cell's rigid shape
4	where the cell reactions take place

2 This table is about the growth of plants.

Match words from the list with each of the numbers 1–4 in the table.

potassium　　**sugars**
nitrates　　**carbon dioxide**

	Use in plants
1	combines with water during photosynthesis
2	used to help make proteins in growth
3	used to build cellulose for cell walls
4	helps to make enzymes used to control photosynthesis

3 The diagram shows an example of an automatic response.

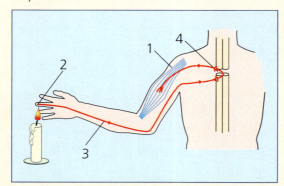

Choose words from the list for each of the labels 1–4 on the diagram.

relay neurone　　**sensory neurone**
effector　　**receptor**

4 Which **two** of the following parts help focus light in the eye?

　　A optic nerve
　　B retina
　　C pupil
　　D cornea
　　E lens

5 The **two** hormones controlling sugar in the blood are:

　　A phosphate
　　B glucagon
　　C ADH
　　D glycogen
　　E insulin

6 This is a diagram of the eye.

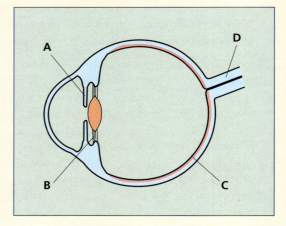

1. Which of the parts is muscular and controls the amount of light entering the eye?

　　A B C D

2. Which part contains light sensitive cells?

　　A B C D

3. Which part of the eye is called the iris?

　　A B C D

4. Which part holds the lens in place?

　　A B C D

7 This plant is photosynthesising.

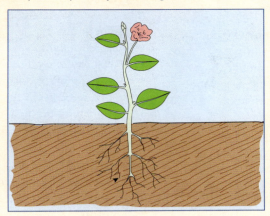

1. If the plant is stunted with yellow older leaves, what would you add to the soil?
    A nitrate
    B potassium
    C sulphate
    D phosphate

2. If the plant developed poor roots with purple leaves, what would you add to the soil?
    A potassium
    B sulphate
    C phosphate
    D nitrate

3. Which of the following substances is necessary for protein synthesis in the plant?
    A potassium
    B calcium
    C phosphate
    D nitrate

4. What is the use of potassium in a plant?
    A it helps the enzymes controlling photosynthesis and respiration
    B it helps to convert starch to sugar
    C it helps to make proteins
    D it allows osmosis to take place more efficiently

8 This question is about water uptake and transport in plants.

1. Carbon dioxide moves into the leaf by:
    A osmosis
    B transpiration
    C diffusion
    D evaporation

2. The evaporation of water from a leaf is known as:
    A transpiration
    B osmosis
    C condensation
    D diffusion

3. More water will evaporate from a leaf on a:
    A hot, dry, windy day
    B cool, dry, calm day
    C hot, dry, calm day
    D hot, humid, windy day

4. Osmosis is *best* described as:
    A movement of water into a sugar solution
    B movement of small particles from a high to a low concentration
    C movement of sugar molecules to balance the concentration of two solutions
    D the nett movement of water from a higher to a lower concentration of water

Competition and survival

Organisms have features (**adaptations**) to help them survive and reproduce in the places where they usually live. For example, body size and surface area affect how much heat an animal can retain, as does the thickness of an insulating coat and the amount of body fat. These adaptations are important for animals in arctic conditions (for example, polar bears).

Camouflage is another adaptation of some plants and animals. Prey use camouflage to avoid being caught, and predators so that prey don't see them coming.

Plants living in dry areas have adaptations that reduce water loss, such as waxy surfaces to their leaves, needles instead of leaves (for example, a cactus) and stomata that are sheltered from the wind to reduce transpiration.

Plants **compete** with other plants in the same habitat for space, water and nutrients from the soil. For example, a new seedling trying to grow under an oak tree is likely to die. Animals compete for space, food and water. For example, birds protect their own territories so they have enough space to breed and food to eat.

The size of a population may be affected by:

- the total amount of food or nutrients available
- competition for food or nutrients
- competition for light
- predation or grazing
- disease.

In a **community**, the size of a population of animals is usually limited by the amount of food available. Changes to one population affect other populations in the community.

If the population of prey (for example, mice) increases, more food is available for predators (for example, owls), so the numbers of predators may increase too.

If the population of predators increases, more food is needed, so the population of of prey may decrease (for example, more owls will eat more mice).

> Physical factors that may affect organisms include:
> - temperature
> - amount of light
> - availability of water
> - availability of oxygen and carbon dioxide.
>
> These vary with the time of day and time of year.

> Animals that kill and eat other animals are **predators**. The animals they eat are called **prey**.

> **Population** – the total number of that type of organism in an area (for example, the number of badgers in a wood).
>
> **Community** – all of the organisms living in a particular area (for example, all of the organisms, including plants, living in a pond).

Relationships within a community

There are different ways of showing how communities of plants and animals are organised:

- **Food chains** show which organisms eat other organisms.

grass → rabbit → fox

A food chain

- **Food webs** show several food chains connected together.
- **Pyramids of numbers** show the number of organisms at each stage of a food chain. The shape of the pyramid doesn't always give a true picture of a food chain.

The source of energy for all organisms in a community is radiation (heat and light) from the Sun. Plants (**producers**) capture a small part of the Sun's energy during photosynthesis. This produces food, which is stored in the cells of the plant and eaten by animals in the next link in the food chain (the **primary consumers**). These animals are themselves eaten by **secondary consumers** higher up in the food chain.

Food chains and webs show us how energy and material is transferred from one organism to another.

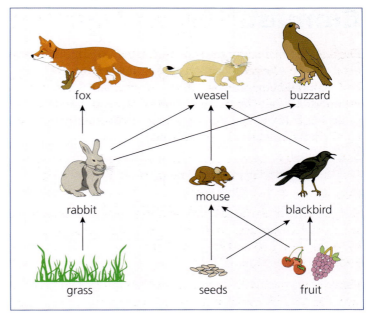

A food web

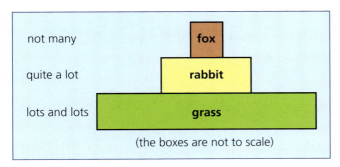

A pyramid of numbers

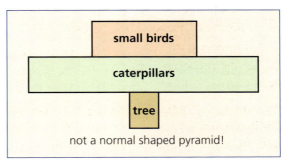

Another pyramid of numbers

Questions

1. Kestrels hunt for mice along the side of a road. What is the predator and what is the prey?

2. One year there are a lot of mice. What is likely to happen to the kestrel population? What is then likely to happen to the number of mice?

3. Draw a spider diagram to show the different factors that will affect the size of a population of animals. **Animal population** should be at the centre of the diagram.

4. On holiday you see a kestrel hunting for small birds and mice in the hedgerow. The mice are eating seeds from some flowers and the birds are eating berries from the hedge and some of the seeds. Draw a simple food web to show this.

Biomass

Biomass is the mass of living material in a community. It can be used to give a better idea than a pyramid of numbers of the energy and material being transferred up a food chain. Compare the two pyramids below. The tree is a single organism that feeds many caterpillars. If you think of it in terms of biomass, you get a better idea of how much energy it supplies.

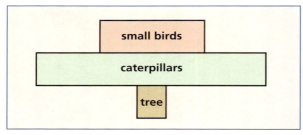

Another pyramid of numbers

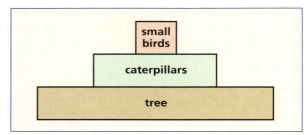

A pyramid of biomass

Losing mass through a food chain

It can be seen that as you go along the food chain less material (biomass) is contained in the organisms. There are a number of reasons for this.

All organisms use materials in respiration to release energy. The energy is used for growth and movement, and much is lost as heat to the surroundings or is excreted. Heat loss is particularly great in mammals and birds, whose bodies need to be kept at a constant temperature, which is often higher than their surroundings.

The efficiency of food production (in other words, reducing losses) can be improved by:

- reducing the number of stages in the food chain (for example, humans eating cereal grain is more efficient than feeding grain to cattle then eating the cattle)

- using hormones to control when fruit ripens on the plant and during transport to supermarkets, so it is just ripe when customers buy it

- reducing the losses from animals by restricting their movement and controlling the temperature they are kept in (for example, by keeping calves in crates to produce veal, the calves do not use up much energy in movement or by trying to keep warm).

This last point is, of course, a very contentious issue.

We can now manage food production very well. In many ways this is good. We can have the food ready for when we want it and we can make sure that it is disease-free and looks good. However, this can mean using hormones and other chemicals, which are suspected not to be good for humans to consume. We have to be very careful in weighing up the advantages and disadvantages of using these chemicals.

Waste and decay

Living things use materials from the environment for growth and other processes (such as respiration, reproduction and repair). All these materials are eventually returned to the environment, either as waste or when organisms die and decay.

All organisms produce waste. For example, trees shed their leaves, which fall to the ground. Some animals excrete urine and defaecate. The organisms themselves, when they die, become waste. The breakdown of this waste is called **decay** and is brought about by **microorganisms** (bacteria and fungi). The process of decay releases substances that plants need to grow.

Microorganisms digest waste material faster in warm, moist conditions. Some microorganisms are more active when there is a rich supply of oxygen. They use the energy released by digestion to drive their own life processes.

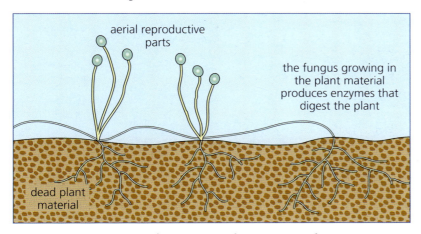

aerial reproductive parts

the fungus growing in the plant material produces enzymes that digest the plant

dead plant material

In a stable community of organisms, the processes that remove materials (for example, plants growing and animals eating plants) are balanced by processes that return materials (decay by microorganisms). The materials are constantly being recycled.

We can use microorganisms to break down dead plant material in compost heaps, producing compost, which we can use to fertilise our gardens. On a larger scale, sewage works use microorganisms to decompose faeces and provide fertilisers. Such uses help to recycle materials that would otherwise be lost. Without recycling, all of the Earth's materials would soon be used up.

Questions

1 Why does a pyramid of biomass usually give us more accurate information than a pyramid of numbers about what is happening to the energy in a community?

2 How is energy lost between the stages of a food chain?

3 Why is it important that the processes that remove materials from our environment are balanced by processes that replace these same materials?

What happens to the waste?

Microorganisms break down dead organisms, both plants and animals. This process of **decay** releases materials that can be used again by other living organisms. The materials are continuously recycled.

There are two important cycles that you must learn. These are the **carbon cycle** and the **nitrogen cycle**.

The carbon cycle · · · · · · · · · · · · · · · · ·

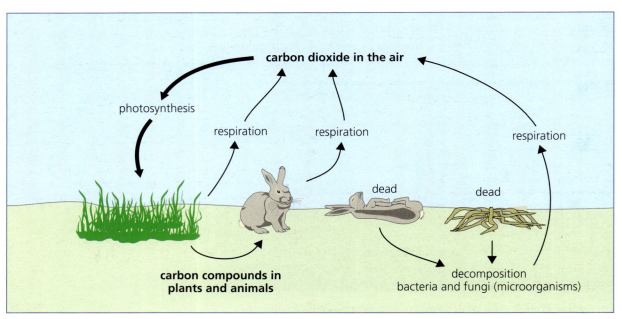

The carbon cycle

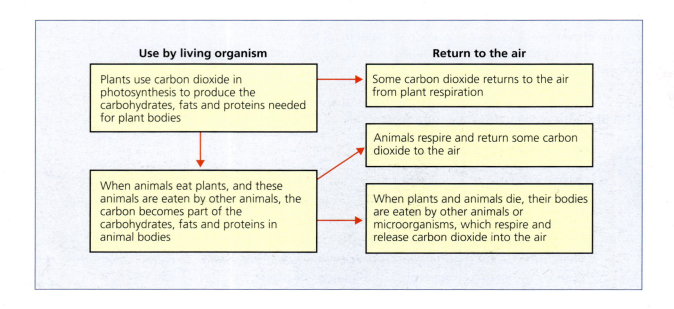

Use by living organism	Return to the air
Plants use carbon dioxide in photosynthesis to produce the carbohydrates, fats and proteins needed for plant bodies	Some carbon dioxide returns to the air from plant respiration
When animals eat plants, and these animals are eaten by other animals, the carbon becomes part of the carbohydrates, fats and proteins in animal bodies	Animals respire and return some carbon dioxide to the air
	When plants and animals die, their bodies are eaten by other animals or microorganisms, which respire and release carbon dioxide into the air

The nitrogen cycle

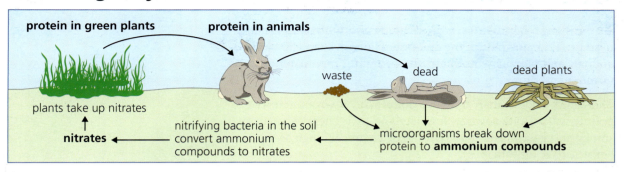

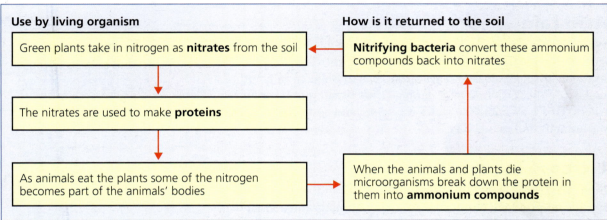

By the time putrefying bacteria and other detritus feeders have broken down all the waste and dead bodies, and all the carbon compounds and proteins have been recycled, then all the energy originally captured by plants has been transferred.

Putrefying bacteria are bacteria that cause decay.

If a community of organisms is **stable**, the processes of decay return as many materials (for example, carbon and nitrogen) to living organisms as they need. The processes that use carbon and nitrogen are balanced by the processes that return them.

Questions

1 Copy and complete these sentences about the carbon cycle using words from the list. You will have to use one of the words more than once:

respiring   decomposing   photosynthesising

Carbon enters the carbon cycle through organisms that are _____. Organisms release carbon back into the cycle as they are _____. Dead, _____ organisms also release carbon back into the atmosphere as they are broken down by bacteria that are _____.

2 In what food types can carbon be found?

3 How is the nitrogen in animals and plants returned to the soil after the organisms have died?

How do humans affect the environment?

As the human population increases more and more land is being used up. Humans reduce the amount of land available for other animals and plants by building, quarrying (for raw materials), farming and dumping waste.

These and other human activities pollute the environment. We pollute water (with sewage, fertiliser and toxic chemicals), air (with smoke and gases), and land (with toxic chemicals such as herbicides and pesticides).

Acid rain

When we burn fossil fuels (that is coal, oil and gas) we release carbon dioxide into the atmosphere. Sulphur dioxide and nitrogen are also released. These gases can dissolve in rain and make it acidic. This rain may damage trees or fall into lakes and rivers. This may make the water too acidic and as a consequence the animals and plants die.

Acid conditions can kill plants and animals because enzymes work only in very specific pH conditions.

Increase in population

In the past there were not enough humans (or industry) to cause a significant problem. Now there are many humans and a great deal of industry across the world. This means that:

- the Earth's raw materials, including fossil fuels (which are non-renewable) are being used up quickly
- we produce much more waste, which, unless we deal with it properly, pollutes our surroundings.

Fertilisers

These are added to the land by farmers to replace the nutrients that plants take up for growth. However, some is washed into lakes, ponds and rivers by rain. This results in **eutrophication**. This means that:

- the water plants grow quickly
- some plants die as a result of increased competition (those below the surface may receive little light because of the large numbers growing on the surface)
- microorganisms (bacteria and fungi) break the dead plants down and use up the oxygen by respiring
- animals will die (suffocate) because of a lack of oxygen.

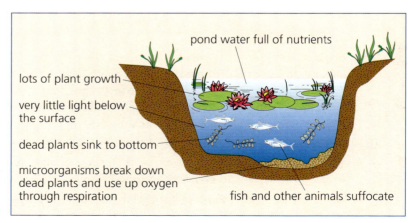

pond water full of nutrients

lots of plant growth

very little light below the surface

dead plants sink to bottom

microorganisms break down dead plants and use up oxygen through respiration

fish and other animals suffocate

Eutrophication in a pond

You might think that with so many plants photosynthesising there would be a lot of oxygen (as the waste product) for fish to use. However, it is all used up by the respiring microorganisms. Untreated sewage in rivers and streams causes the same problem because the microorganisms break it down and use up the oxygen.

The Greenhouse Effect

Tropical forests are being cut down on a large scale. This is called **deforestation**. The wood may be used for timber and the land for agriculture. This has several results.

- If the wood is burned then carbon dioxide is released as a product of combustion.
- If the wood is left to decay then the respiring microorganisms release carbon dioxide.
- Fewer trees use less carbon dioxide to photosynthesise so less carbon is 'locked up' in wood and the carbon cycle is disturbed.

Carbon dioxide in the atmosphere is also released by the burning of fossils fuels (for example, coal for power stations, petrol by cars). Methane gas is released into the atmosphere by cattle and by rice fields.

The levels of these two gases are rising. They act like a blanket, trapping some of the Sun's energy, which would normally be reflected back out of our atmosphere. So the temperature of the Earth increases. This is known as the 'Greenhouse Effect'.

A rise in temperature of a few degrees Centigrade may cause:

- significant changes in the Earth's climate
- a rise in the level of the sea.

All the issues described on these pages are environmental problems that everyone must face. We must find ways of balancing the needs of the world's growing population with the need to protect our planet for future generations. This is called **sustainable development**.

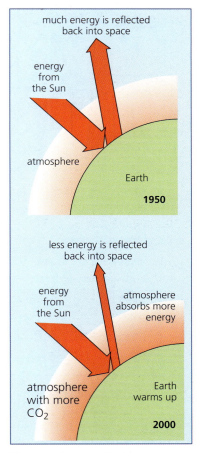

The greenhouse effect

Questions

1 How can burning fossil fuels destroy life in a lake?

2 If too much fertiliser gets into a pond, why might all of the animals die?

3 Why is there more carbon dioxide in the air now than there was 100 years ago?

4 We are now able to buy foods from all around the world in our shops. However, these are often transported by aeroplane. Aeroplanes produce a large amount of 'Greenhouse gases' when flying. Do you think that the choice we have in food is worth the effect this has on our environment?

Terminal exam questions

1 The diagram below shows a food web for a wood.

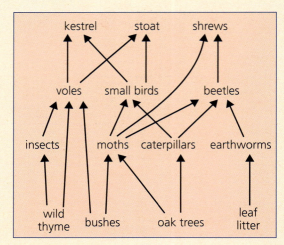

a These diagrams show a pyramid of numbers and a pyramid of biomass for the same wood.

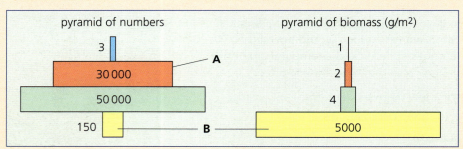

  i Name one organism from the level labelled A. [1]

  ii Explain, as fully as you can, why the level labelled B is such a different width in the two pyramids. [3]

b The plants in the wood capture the Sun's energy. Explain, as fully as you can, what happens to this energy. [8]

c Leaf litter is decomposing leaves. Explain, as fully as you can, how nitrogen (found as protein in the leaves) will eventually be found in other plants. [5]

d How is energy lost between the stages in a food chain? [4]

21 marks

2 Over a number of years a farmer uses fertiliser on his fields. Eventually he notices that one of the ponds is becoming full of plants. What is likely to happen in the pond over the next few years? [6]

6 marks

3 The Greenhouse Effect is thought to be an increasing problem on the planet.

a **i** Name **two** 'Greenhouse' gases. [2]

  ii Why are these gases increasing in the atmosphere? [3]

  iii How is the Greenhouse Effect brought about? [3]

b **i** Name **two** gases that cause acid rain. [2]

  ii Explain the problems that acid rain causes. [4]

14 marks

4 The diagram below shows a food web

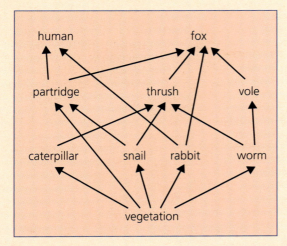

a Draw a food chain, of four organisms, from this food web [1]

b i Name the producer in this food web. [1]

ii What is likely to happen to the vole population if the number of worms increases? Explain your answer. [3]

iii What is likely to happen to the number of caterpillars if the number of snails falls? [4]

c Give four factors that will affect the size of an animal population [4]

13 marks

5 Here is a diagram of the carbon cycle.

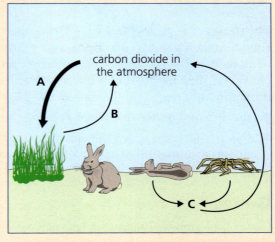

a i What process is taking place at A? [1]

ii Name **three** types of substance that the plants may produce as a result of this process. [3]

b i What process is taking place at B? [1]

ii Name **one** substance (other than carbon dioxide) that is produced as a result of this process. [1]

c Explain fully how carbon dioxide is released from the dead rabbit as indicated by C in the diagram. [4]

d Give **two** problems that the Greenhouse Effect is likely to cause. [2]

12 marks

Total for test: 66 marks

Why are we all different?

The young of a species often have characteristics that are similar to their parents'. This is because information is passed on to them in the sex cells from which they have developed. However, all individuals in a species are actually different. These differences are due a combination of two factors:

- the different **genes** that they have inherited (**genetic causes**)
- the conditions in which they have developed or been brought up (**environmental causes**).

'Species' means a type of organism. Members of the same species can breed with each other.

Genes

Genes are found within the nucleus of a cell. The nucleus contains **chromosomes** that are made up of many genes. Each gene controls some particular characteristic of the body (for example, eye colour). The chromosomes are found in pairs. The number of chromosome pairs in body cells is different for each species. Human body cells have 23 pairs, making 46 chromosomes in all.

Both chromosomes in each pair are made up of genes that usually control the same characteristics. This means that the genes themselves are usually paired. Some genes have different forms – these are called **alleles**.

These alleles control the same characteristics but may carry different information about them. For example, in the pair of alleles controlling eye colour, there is one allele for blue and one allele for brown.

In sexual reproduction these chromosomes are regularly shuffled so that each individual has a unique combination of alleles.

Sexual reproduction

In sexual reproduction a male sex cell and a female sex cell join together. In humans these are the sperm and the egg. Sex cells are also called **gametes**.

Sex cells are formed by cells in the reproductive organs (ovaries and testes in humans), which divide to form cells that have one from each pair of chromosomes. This process is called **meiosis**.

Asexual reproduction

No sex cells are involved in asexual reproduction, so the genetic information in the offspring is exactly the same as that of the parent. This type of reproduction is most common in plants (for example, new plants growing from runners, tubers or bulbs). The offspring are called **clones**. The type of cell division used in asexual reproduction is called **mitosis**.

Gregor Mendel

Mendel was the first person to discover the scientific clue to the way that characteristics are inherited. In the 1850s he carried out some experiments with garden peas. By selecting and mating tall peas and short peas in different combinations he was able to work out that these characteristics are inherited by a special 'factors' we now call **genes**. It took another 100 years for scientists to discover genes and prove Mendel's **law of inheritance**.

In asexual reproduction new individuals are produced through mitosis.

Mitosis

Before cell division, a copy of each chromosome is made so that when the cell divides each new cell has exactly the same genetic information. This type of cell division is called **mitosis**. The diagram shows what happens.

Mitosis takes place all the time, to enable an organism to grow and to replace cells that have died. For example, skin cells are continually wearing off and being replaced.

There is an almost infinite number of combinations of genes, and so an infinite number of possibilities for new individuals. This is why sexual reproduction gives rise to variation (the differences between individuals).

The new cell, formed when the gametes fuse, then divides again and again by **mitosis** to form a new individual.

Cell division – mitosis

Meiosis

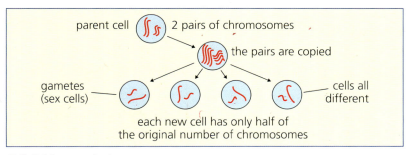

Cell division – meiosis.

Cells in the reproductive organs, as in the rest of the body, have one pair of each type of chromosome. At the start of meiosis a copy of each chromosome is made, so that there are two pairs of each.

The cell now divides twice to make four sex cells. Each of these sex cells (gametes) has one copy of each chromosome. In humans, this is 23 chromosomes.

When the male and female gametes join at fertilisation their single chromosomes combine, making a cell with its full number of chromosomes (46 in humans). New pairs of chromosomes and genes have been formed in the new cell, so that the new individual will be different.

Questions

1 What are the **two** factors causing variation between members of the same species?

2 How does a cell with 23 pairs of chromosomes divide to produce four new sex cells, with only half the number of chromosomes?

3 Why are organisms produced by asexual reproduction identical to the parent?

4 Turkeys have 82 chromosomes (in 41 pairs) in their cells. How many chromosomes do their gametes have?

Controlling reproduction

As gardeners know, new plants can be produced quickly and cheaply by taking cuttings from existing plants. These plants will be exactly the same, genetically, as the parent plant. To grow successfully, they need a warm, moist atmosphere until the roots develop.

Artificial selection

We can choose those individuals with the best characteristics to breed from (for example, the fastest male and female horses). This **selective breeding** is now a very big industry. A great range of plants and animals are being 'improved' in this way.

However, selective breeding reduces the variety of alleles in a population. This is because individuals without the alleles that are desired are not used to breed, so the alleles may eventually be lost. If the environment changes, new diseases may evolve and suitable alleles may not be there to help the species survive. For example, some alleles in a species may prevent a particular disease. If individuals are bred only for their meat quality, then some of these alleles may be lost along the way. It would then be difficult for the species to adapt to combat the disease should it break out.

As an alternative, modern **cloning** (a type of artificial selection) can involve:

- **tissue culture** – using small groups of cells from part of a plant to grow into a new plant
- **embryo transplants** – splitting cells from a developing embryo and transplanting into a 'host' parent (this must be done before the cells become specialised).

Dolly the sheep made headline news in 1997. She was the first animal to be cloned from adult cells. She is an identical copy of her genetic mother, but has no father!

Genetic engineering

Genes from one species can be 'cut out' of a chromosome and transferred to another species (for example, a bacterium). The transferred gene continues to make the same protein in its new 'home'.

This technique can be used on a large scale to manufacture drugs and homones. For example, the production of **insulin** for diabetics is now carried out in this way by bacteria.

It is also possible to transfer genes to 'host' organisms at an early stage of development to give 'better' characteristics (for example, genetically modified tomatoes).

What do you think?
There are many advantages to cloning and genetic engineering. Producing pest-resistant crops and cows that produce more milk makes economic sense for farmers, and helps feed people in poorer countries. Genetically modified (GM) plants can be produced, which are resistant to disease.
But are GM foods safe to eat? What effects do they have on the environment? If we can clone sheep, what about cloning humans? Would this be morally right? Who decides what sort of people are 'desirable' and 'not desirable'?
Scientists, politicians and we the public have to look at all the advantages and disadvantages when deciding what is the best way to use these new techniques.

How can women control their fertility?

An egg is released every month. The thickness of the lining of the womb (uterus) increases during the month. These changes are controlled by hormones secreted by the pituitary gland (at the base of the brain) and by the ovaries.

Fertility in women can be controlled by:

■ hormones that stimulate (encourage) eggs to be produced (fertility drugs)

■ hormones that stop eggs being released from the ovaries (the pill).

Several hormones are involved in the menstrual cycle. The hormones controlling egg release include:

■ **follicle stimulating hormone** (FSH) secreted by the pituitary gland – this causes the eggs to mature and ovaries to produce oestrogens

■ **oestrogen** secreted by the ovaries – inhibits (stops) more production of FSH, which stops more eggs maturing; it also causes the pituitary gland to produce luteinising hormone (LH)

■ **luteinising hormone** – causes the release of an egg mid-way through the menstral cycle.

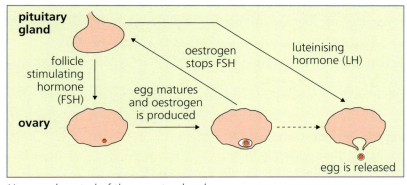

Hormonal control of the menstrual cycle

FSH can be used as a fertility drug if a woman's own production of FSH is too low. Oestrogen can be taken (as an oral contraceptive) to stop FSH production so no eggs are released.

Questions

1 Describe **one** example of genetic engineering.

2 A small animal in South America is near extinction. Scientists start a breeding programme using only the most attractive animals. The number of animals in the population rises. A disease strikes the population and the scientists are unable to save the animals, which then die out. Another scientist says that it was our fault the animal became extinct. How could she explain her statement?

3 What is meant by cloning? What type of cell division does it involve?

4 Women who cannot produce eggs can be given fertility treatment. Suggest advantages and disadvantages of this treatment.

Inheritance in humans

What are chromosomes?

Chromosomes are made of long molecules of **DNA** (deoxyribonucleic acid). Genes are shorter lengths of DNA within the chromosomes. DNA contains the coded information that determines inherited characteristics.

DNA is made of long strands of four different molecules called **bases**. A sequence of three of these bases codes for a particular amino acid. This means that the order of the bases controls the order of amino acids that join together to form a protein. In other words, a specific length of DNA will produce a specific protein. It is these proteins that determine our characteristics.

Inheritance

Genetic characteristics are controlled by pairs of genes. The genes in these pairs often have two alleles (alternative forms).

One of these alleles is the **dominant** form. That is, when it appears in the pair it determines the characteristic that the pair of genes controls.

For example, **Huntington's chorea** (a disorder of the nervous system) is controlled by a dominant allele (H) – if you have the allele you will develop the disorder. So it can be inherited from one parent who has the disorder.

The other allele is **recessive** (h). If it appears in a pair with the dominant allele, it does not control the characteristic linked to that gene. It is only when both alleles are recessive that their effects show and Huntington's chorea does not develop.

For example, **cystic fibrosis** (a disorder of the cell membranes) is carried only by recessive alleles (c), so both alleles must be recessive for the individual to develop the disorder. This means that both parents must carry the recessive allele.

If individuals have two identical alleles for a characteristic, whether these are dominant or recessive, they are said to be **homozygous** (for example, cc). If they have a dominant and recessive allele, they are **heterozygous** (for example, Hh).

You can use genetic diagrams to show the inheritance of dominant and recessive alleles clearly. The two alleles are shown by the same letter, but dominant alleles have a capital.

Worked example

Q One heterozygous parent and one homozygous recessive parent for Huntington's chorea have a child. What is the chance of the child developing the disorder?

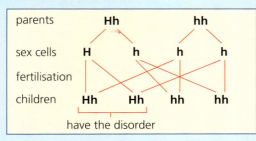

A The chance is one in two.

Q Two heterozygous parents for cystic fibrosis have a child. What is the chance of the child having cyctic fibrosis

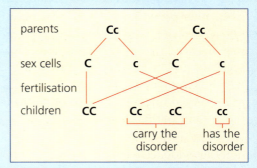

A The chance is one in four.

In **sickle cell anaemia** (a disorder of the red blood cells) the disorder is carried by a recessive allele (s). Being heterozygous (Ss) helps to protect against malaria. This means that carrying the disorder can be an advantage in countries where malaria is common.

Determining sex

We have 23 pairs of chromosomes. One of these pairs determines the sex we are. In females the sex cells are the same (called XX because of their shape). In males they are different (called XY because of their shape). So eggs always have an X chromosome while sperm may carry an X chromosome or a Y chromosome.

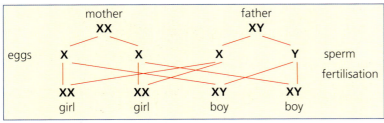

There is a 50% chance of having a boy and a 50% chance of having a girl

Worked example

Q Two parents who are heterozygous for sickle cell anaemia (so do not show symptoms) have a child. What is the chance that the child will develop the disorder?

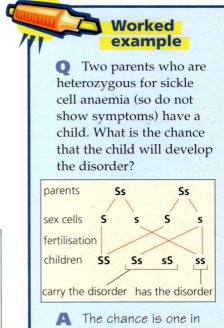

A The chance is one in four

Questions

1 One parent is heterozygous for sickle cell anaemia, the other homozygous (dominant). What is the chance of their children being carriers of the disorder? You should use a genetic diagram.

2 Two parents do not have Huntington's chorea. What is the chance, if any, of their children having the disorder?

Natural selection

Evidence for evolution

Fossils are found in rocks. They are the remains of plants and animals that lived a very long time ago. They were formed:

■ from the hard parts of animals that did not decay easily

■ from other parts that did not decay because of lack of oxygen

■ when parts of the organism were replaced by other materials as they decayed (for example, chemicals may dissolve out of seashells and be replaced by minerals such as iron or silicon, which then preserve the shape).

■ as preserved traces of animals or plants (for example, footprints, burrows or rootlet traces).

Fossils show us how species have changed over millions of years. From fossil evidence we now know that all of the species today developed from simple life forms that existed over three billion years ago.

> Darwin argued that all species, including humans, can be traced back to more primitive species, and eventually back to the first organisms. This was highly controversial because of the teachings of the Church at that time. Many people believed quite literally that humans were descended from Adam, who was put on the Earth as a 'ready-made' human by God. It took many years for Darwin's theory to be accepted.

Theories of Evolution

In 1809 Lamarck proposed that there could be major changes leading to new species appearing almost immediately in response to the necessity for a species to survive. So, for example, if food was scarce then giraffes would need to reach up higher for leaves to eat. This would stretch their necks, and this characteristic would be passed on to the next generation.

Fifty years later, Darwin showed that these changes happen only gradually by a series of small changes in response to survival in the environment. He argued that there will always be more giraffes born than food available. Those that happen to have longer necks would be more likely to survive and reproduce. So the characteristic for long necks would gradually be passed on through generations, until eventually all giraffes have long necks. Darwin called this **natural selection**.

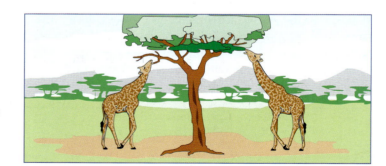

Natural selection

Natural selection can be summarised like this:

■ **species** – there is wide variation in any species

■ **victims** – predation, disease and competition for food kill some

■ **survivors** – those best suited to their environment survive (for example, the faster, best camouflaged or most resistant to disease)

■ **selection** – these breed and the alleles are passed to the next generation.

> Natural selection favours individuals in a species that are best adapted to survive and therefore breed

An example of natural selection can be seen today. Antibiotics are used to help cure humans of infections caused by bacteria. Some bacteria survive these antibiotics and breed. This means that over a period of time bacteria become resistant to the antibiotics, and so the antibiotics are no longer useful for fighting infection. This is why doctors try not to prescribe antibiotics for illnesses unless really necessary.

How do new species evolve?

Genes may change because of **mutation**. Mutations occur naturally but the chances of one can be increased by:

- exposure to ionising radiations, such as ultraviolet light, X-rays and other forms of radiation
- exposure to some chemicals.

Most mutations are harmful:

- reproductive cells may become abnormal or die
- body cells may multiply out of control, and the effect may spread to other parts of the body – this is **cancer**.

Some mutations have no effect and some may even *increase* the chance of survival. These are the mutations that give rise to new species through natural selection.

How do species die out?

Species need to be able to adapt to changes. For example:

- their environment may change (for example, climate, availability of food)
- new predators may evolve, or new diseases, that can kill them
- another species may evolve that competes with them (for example, for food).

If evolution does not occur so species can adapt to survive these changes, they will eventually become extinct.

Questions

1 Fully preserved specimens of insects that are thousands of years old have been found preserved in amber (solidified sap). Explain why they are so well preserved.

2 Give **three** different causes of mutation.

3 There are **two** varieties of peppered moth in Britain, pale and dark. Pale moths are found in rural areas where tree trunks are mottled grey. Dark moths are found in industrial areas where tree trunks are blackened. Suggest how this distribution might have come about.

4 Draw a spider diagram to show the different ways a species might become extinct. **Extinction** should be at the centre of the diagram.

5 Antibiotics always used to cure diseases caused by bacteria. Why is this no longer the case?

Terminal exam questions

1 a State **two** differences between meiosis and mitosis. [2]

b Plants are often reproduced asexually by taking cuttings.
Why are new plants exactly the same as their parents? [2]

c i What is meant by selective breeding? [3]

ii Selective breeding is thought to be a good idea in the short term. What problems may arise in the long term if this process continues? [4]

11 marks

2 a i What is meant by the term 'genetic engineering?' [1]

ii How is the process carried out? [3]

iii Give **one** example of genetic engineering. [3]

b What is meant by the term 'heterozygous'? [3]

c i What body system does Huntington's chorea affect? [1]

ii Two parents are both heterozygous for Huntington's chorea.
If they decide to have a child, what is the chance of him/her having the disorder? [4]

15 marks

3 a i Name **two** methods of cloning. [2]

ii For each of the methods you have given, explain what actually takes place. [4]

b Two parents decide to have a child. The father is heterozygous for the disorder of cystic fibrosis and the mother does not carry a gene for the disorder.
What is the chance of the child having the disorder? [4]

10 marks

4 Explain the process of Natural Selection. [5]

5 marks

5 a i What is meant by the term dominant? [1]

ii What are alleles? [2]

b i Study this diagram of meiosis.

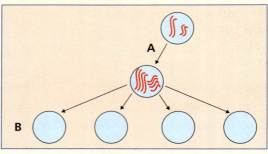

• What is happening at A? [1]
• Copy the diagram and complete the cells at B, showing the results of meiosis. [2]

ii What function does meiosis serve? [1]

c i A man heterozygous for sickle cell anaemia marries a homozygous 'normal' woman. They have a child. What is the chance of the child:
• showing symptoms of the disease?
• carrying the disease? [5]

ii What is the possible advantage in being heterozygous for sickle cell anaemia? [1]

b How do chromosomes control the characteristics we actually have? [4]

17 marks

6 a Study this diagram of human egg production.

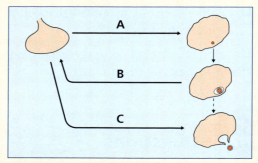

i Explain what is happening at A, B and C. Name the hormones involved. [6]

ii Which gland (in the brain) is responsible for the production of certain sex hormones? [1]

b i Which hormone is used to increase fertility? [1]

ii Which hormone is used in the birth control pill? [1]

9 marks

Total for test: 67 marks

Materials and their properties

Metals

Earth materials

Patterns of chemical change

Structures and bonding

The periodic table

All of the elements are arranged in rows, in order of their relative atomic masses. Elements in the same columns have similar properties. Elements in the same column are known as a **Group**. The whole arrangement is known as the **periodic table**.

Examples of metals include:

■ sodium and potassium in Group 1

■ magnesium and calcium in Group 2.

There are a few elements that do not fit this pattern. For example, argon has a greater atomic mass than potassium but because of its properties it is better placed before potassium in the table. So argon is placed in Group 0.

More than three-quarters of all elements are metals. In the periodic table most metals are found:

■ in the two left-hand columns (Groups 1 and 2)

■ in the central block (transition metals)

Li lithium	Be berylium		
Na sodium	Mg magnesium		
K potassium	Ca calcium	Transition metals	
Rb rubidium	Sr strontium		
Cs caesium	Ba barium		
Fr francium	Ra radium		

Group 1 metals

The elements in Group 1 are known as the **alkali metals** because they form hydroxides that dissolve in water to form alkaline solutions.

The alkali metals:

■ have a low density (the first three are less dense than water and will float as they react)

■ react with non-metals to form ionic compounds. These compounds will then dissolve in water to form colourless solutions. For example:

potassium + oxygen ⟶ potassium oxide

■ react with water to give off hydrogen. For example:

sodium + water ⟶ sodium hydroxide + hydrogen

■ react with water to form hydroxides that dissolve in the water to form alkaline solutions (such as sodium hydroxide in the equation above).

Transition metals

These metals are in the centre of the periodic table. They include copper and iron. Like all metals, the transition metals:

■ are good conductors of heat

■ are good conductors of electricity

■ can easily be bent or hammered into different shapes.

However, they are different to the alkali metals in Group 1. Transition metals:

- have high melting points (all except for mercury, which has a low melting point and is a liquid even at room temperature)
- are much harder, tougher and stronger
- are not nearly as reactive as the alkali metals so they do not react (corrode) as quickly with either water or oxygen.

These properties make transition metals very useful. For example, **iron** is used (usually in the form of steel) for making structures, such as girders in buildings or in bridges. **Copper** is used for making things that either transfer heat (such as the bottoms of pans for cooking) or transfer electricity (such as wires).

Most of the transition metals form coloured compounds. These compounds can be seen in the coloured glazes on pottery, and when copper has been weathered (it turns green).

Some transition metals, for example iron and **platinum**, are used as catalysts (chemicals that speed up reactions).

Which metals are the most reactive? ● ● ●

We can tell by looking at how quickly they react:
- with air to produce metal oxides, for example:

  magnesium + oxygen → magnesium oxide

  $$2Mg + O_2 \rightarrow 2MgO$$

- with water (cold, hot or as steam) to produce metal hydroxides or oxides and hydrogen, for example:

  calcium + water → calcium hydroxide + hydrogen

  $$Ca + 2H_2O \rightarrow Ca(OH)_2 + H_2$$

- with dilute acids to produce metal salts and hydrogen, for example:

  zinc + hydrochloric acid → zinc chloride + hydrogen

  $$Zn + 2HCl \rightarrow ZnCl_2 + H_2$$

The most reactive metals are at the top of the reactivity list. A more reactive metal will displace a less reactive metal from its compounds.

For example, aluminium is more reactive than iron so ...

aluminium + iron(III) oxide → iron + aluminium oxide

$$2Al + Fe_2O_3 \rightarrow 2Fe + Al_2O_3$$

Comparing the reactions of different metals helps us to complete a **reactivity series**.

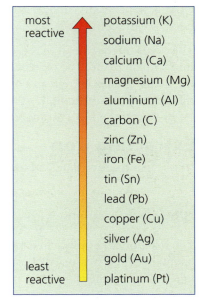

most reactive	potassium (K)
	sodium (Na)
	calcium (Ca)
	magnesium (Mg)
	aluminium (Al)
	carbon (C)
	zinc (Zn)
	iron (Fe)
	tin (Sn)
	lead (Pb)
	copper (Cu)
	silver (Ag)
	gold (Au)
least reactive	platinum (Pt)

Some metals in order of reactivity

Carbon is not a metal, but we include it in the reactivity series because it behaves like a metal in a way that makes it useful for extracting other metals from their ores (see page 44).

Questions

1. Name **two** elements in Group 1 of the periodic table.
2. Are elements with similar properties found in rows or groups?
3. Zinc is added to copper chloride solution. Predict and explain what would happen.
4. Metals have a number of properties. Draw a spider diagram to show **three** of these properties. **Properties of metals** should be at the centre of the diagram.
5. Mercury is a good conductor of electricity. Why is it never used for electrical wires?

Extracting the metals from their ores

A more reactive element will displace a less reactive element from its compounds. This principle is used to extract some metals from their ores.

The Earth's crust contains metals and metal compounds. They are usually mixed with other substances to form **ores**. The more reactive the metal, the more difficult it is to extract it from its ore. This is because it readily forms strong compounds with other elements. There must be enough metal in the ore to make it worthwhile extracting it. How it is extracted depends on the reactivity of the metal. Extraction can be chemical or by electrolysis.

Gold is so unreactive that it is found as a pure metal – there is no need to extract it.

The ore is often a metal oxide, or something that is easily changed into a metal oxide. The oxygen, therefore, must be removed to leave the metal. This is known as a **reduction**. The more reactive the metal, the more difficult it is to remove the oxygen.

Extracting iron

Iron is less reactive than carbon so the following reaction is possible:

iron oxide + carbon → iron + carbon dioxide

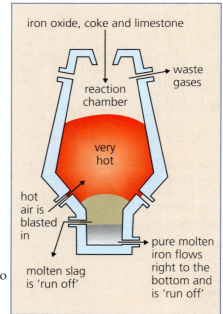

iron oxide, coke and limestone

waste gases

reaction chamber

very hot

hot air is blasted in

molten slag is 'run off'

pure molten iron flows right to the bottom and is 'run off'

The blast furnace

The reaction takes place in a blast furnace. The raw materials are haematite (iron oxide), coke (carbon) and limestone. The reaction takes place in stages:

■ Coke burns in hot air to produce carbon dioxide and lots of heat energy:

carbon + oxygen → carbon dioxide

■ In the heat of the furnace, coke burns with carbon dioxide:

carbon + carbon dioxide → carbon monoxide

■ The carbon monoxide **reduces** the iron oxide in the iron ore. Iron and carbon dioxide are produced. The molten iron flows to the bottom of the furnace. The oxygen reacts with carbon monoxide to produce carbon dioxide. This is called **oxidation**.

■ Overall:

iron oxide + carbon monoxide → iron + carbon dioxide

Acid impurities go to the bottom of the furnace as waste. Limestone is added and reacts with the impurities to form **slag**, which floats on the pure iron and is run off. Molten iron flows from the bottom of the furnace.

Extracting more reactive metals • • • • •

Many metals are more reactive than iron. It takes more energy to extract them from their ores. Aluminium is more reactive and must be extracted by **electrolysis**.

Most reactive metals form ionic compounds, where the metals are positively charged ions. When ionic compounds are either dissolved in water or melted the ions are free to move about and can be separated by passing an electric current through them.

In electrolysis the positive ions are attracted to the negative electrode (cathode) and the negative ions are attracted to the positive electrode (anode). During this process gases can be given off or metals deposited on the electrodes.

Extracting aluminium • • • • • •

The raw materials for producing aluminium are aluminium oxide (purified from the ore **bauxite**) and cryolite. Aluminium oxide has a very high melting point but can be dissolved in molten cryolite at a much lower temperature.

The electrodes are made of carbon. During electrolysis:

- aluminium forms at the negative electrode
- oxygen forms at the positive electrodes where it reacts with the carbon to produce carbon dioxide – this makes the electrodes burn away quickly, so they have to be replaced frequently.

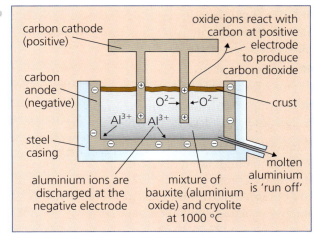

Extracting aluminium by electrolysis

Purifying copper • • • • • • • • • • • • •

Electrolysis can also be used to purify copper.

Copper ions move from the impure copper positive electrode (anode) through a solution containing copper ions to the pure copper negative electrode (cathode). Here they are deposited as pure metal. So the positive electrode gets smaller and the negative electrode grows.

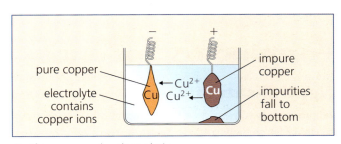

Purifying copper by electrolysis

Questions

1. Why is limestone added in the extraction of iron?
2. Why is carbon **not** used in the extraction of aluminium?
3. Why does the aluminium ore have to be melted before aluminium can be extracted? Why is cryolite used?
4. A company is extracting lead, tin and magnesium from their ores. Which of these metals cannot be extracted using carbon?

Redox reactions

In the extraction of both iron and aluminium, **reduction** and **oxidation** reactions take place. For example, during electrolysis the positively charged aluminium ions gained electrons at the negative electrode (reduction), and the negatively charged oxygen ions lost electrons at the positive electrode (oxidation).

In a chemical reaction, if oxidation occurs then reduction must also occur – because if one ion is losing an electron then another ion must be gaining one. These are called **redox reactions**.

We don't want the metals we extract from ores turning back into to metal oxides (oxidising, or corroding). There are ways of preventing metals doing this.

Iron (or steel) corrodes more quickly than most other transition metals. It reacts with oxygen in the air to produce iron oxide (rust). This can be prevented by:

■ connecting it to a more reactive metal (for example, zinc or magnesium). This is called **sacrificial protection**.

■ mixing it with another metal (for example, chromium) to make an alloy (stainless steel), which does not corrode.

Aluminium does not corrode as quickly as you would expect from its position high up in the reactivity series. This is because the aluminium on the outside reacts with oxygen to make a thin film of aluminium oxide. This quickly covers the rest of the aluminium, so air and water can no longer get to it.

Aluminium is a useful structural metal and can be mixed with other metals (for example, magnesium) to make it harder, stronger and stiffer.

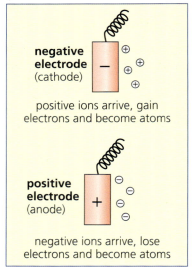

What happens in a redox reaction during electrolysis

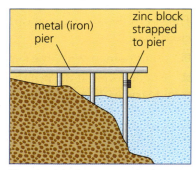

The zinc block prevents the iron pier from rusting

Forming compounds

Neutralisation

Alkali metals (Group 1 of the periodic table) have oxides and hydroxides that dissolve in water to form alkaline solutions. These react with acidic solutions in **neutralisation** reactions to produce salts.

acid + alkali → salt + water

The salt produced depends on:
■ the metal in the alkali
■ the acid used.

Substances can dissolve in water to produce solutions that are acidic, alkaline or neutral. The pH scale is a measure of this.

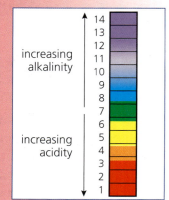

Neutralising hydrochloric acid produces chlorides:

hydrochloric acid + sodium hydroxide → sodium chloride + water

$$HCl + NaOH → NaCl + H_2O$$

Neutralising nitric acid produces nitrates:

nitric acid + sodium hydroxide → sodium nitrate + water

$$HNO_3 + NaOH → NaNO_3 + H_2O$$

Neutralising sulphuric acid produces sulphates:

sulphuric acid + sodium hydroxide → sodium sulphate + water

$$H_2SO_4 + 2NaOH → Na_2SO_4 + 2H_2$$

Hydrogen ions (H^+) make acidic solutions. Hydroxide ions (OH^-) make alkaline solutions. In a neutralisation reaction they react to make water (H_2O), which is neutral:

$$H^+ (aq) + OH^- (aq) → H_2O (l)$$

Ammonia also dissolves in water to form an alkaline solution (ammonium hydroxide). This can also be neutralised to form an ammonium salt.

> In a neutralisation reaction, indicators are used to tell you when the reaction is complete. The salt solution is neutral.

Bases

Unlike the alkali metals, transition metals have oxides and hydroxides that do not dissolve in water – **bases**. You can make a transition metal salt by reacting a base with an acid:

$$acid + base → salt + water$$

You can produce a solution of a soluble transition metal salt by adding the insoluble base to the acid until no more will react, then filtering off the excess base (oxide or hydroxide).

Questions

1 What is a redox reaction?

2 Iron corrodes over a period of time. What conditions will speed up the corrosion of iron?

3 What is meant by a neutralisation reaction?

4 Predict the salts that will result from these neutralisation reactions. Copy and complete the table.

+	hydrochloric acid	sulphuric acid
potassium hydroxide		
calcium hydroxide		

5 Write down the chemical reaction between KOH and HCl.

Module test questions

1 This question is about the reactivities of different elements.

Match words from the list with spaces 1–4.

gold   **aluminium**
carbon   **iron**

most reactive   1 _____
                        2 _____
                        3 _____
least reactive   4 _____

2 This question is about the substances formed during certain chemical reactions.

Match the chemical formulae from the list with each of numbers 1–4 in the table.

NaCl   **NaNO₃**
Na₂SO₄   **Na₂O**

	Reactants
1	hydrochloric acid and sodium hydroxide
2	sodium and oxygen
3	nitric acid and sodium hydroxide
4	sulphuric acid and sodium hydroxide

3 This question is about the different types of chemical reactions.

Match words from the list with each of numbers 1–4 in the table.

displacement   **reduction**
neutralisation   **oxidation**

	Description
1	the reaction between an acid and an alkali
2	when a metal oxide loses its oxygen
3	when a metal becomes a metal oxide
4	when a more reactive metal removes a less reactive metal from a compound

4 When sulphuric acid is neutralised by sodium hydroxide the **two** products of the reaction are:

   A Na_2SO_4
   B H_2
   C H_2O
   D CO_2
   E   NaCl

5 In the electrolysis of aluminium oxide (bauxite), which **two** of the following statements are correct?

   A   cryolite is used to reduce the melting point of the ore
   B   the positive electrode is made of aluminium
   C   oxygen forms at the negative electrode
   D   negative ions gain an electron to form an atom
   E   aluminium forms at the negative electrode

6 This is a diagram of a blast furnace.

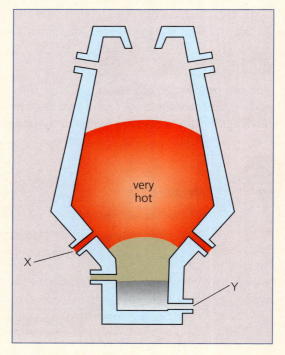

1. What is happening at point X?
   A   waste gases are escaping
   B   molten iron is flowing
   C   hot air is blasted in
   D   molten slag is run off

2. What is happening at point Y?
   - **A** hot air is blasted in
   - **B** molten iron is flowing
   - **C** molten slag is run off
   - **D** limestone is added

3. Which substance reduces iron oxide?
   - **A** carbon monoxide
   - **B** carbon
   - **C** limestone
   - **D** carbon dioxide

4. With which of the following substances does limestone react to form slag?
   - **A** carbon monoxide
   - **B** carbon dioxide
   - **C** acid impurities
   - **D** carbon

7 Aluminium is extracted from its ore by electrolysis.

1. What happens at the negative electrode?
   - **A** negative aluminium ions gain electrons and become atoms
   - **B** negative aluminium ions lose electrons and become atoms
   - **C** positive aluminium ions gain electrons and become atoms
   - **D** positive aluminium ions lose electrons and become atoms

2. What happens at the positive electrode?
   - **A** negative oxygen ions gain electrons and become atoms
   - **B** negative oxygen ions lose electrons and become atoms
   - **C** positive oxygen ions gain electrons and become atoms
   - **D** positive oxygen ions lose electrons and become atoms

3. What happens eventually to the oxygen ions?
   - **A** they evolve as oxygen atoms
   - **B** they evolve as carbon dioxide molecules
   - **C** they form hydroxide (OH) ions
   - **D** they evolve as oxygen molecules

4. What is cryolite used for?
   - **A** to prevent the electrodes breaking down
   - **B** to conduct electricity
   - **C** to provide aluminium ions
   - **D** to lower the melting point of the ore

8 Copper is purified by electrolysis.

1. What happens at the positive electrode?
   - **A** copper atoms lose electrons to become copper ions
   - **B** copper atoms gain electrons to become copper ions
   - **C** copper ions lose electrons to become copper atoms
   - **D** copper ions gain electrons to become copper atoms

2. What happens at the negative electrode?
   - **A** copper atoms lose electrons to become copper ions
   - **B** copper atoms gain electrons to become copper ions
   - **C** copper ions lose electrons to become copper atoms
   - **D** copper ions gain electrons to become copper atoms

3. What is the liquid around the electrodes (the electrolyte)?
   - **A** water
   - **B** an acid
   - **C** a solution containing copper ions
   - **D** an alkali

4. Copper can be found 'native' (as fairly pure metal). Iron oxide can be reduced by carbon to leave iron. Aluminium oxide cannot be reduced by carbon.

   What place does carbon have in the reactivity series of aluminium, carbon, copper and iron?
   - **A** it is the most reactive
   - **B** it is more reactive than copper and iron
   - **C** it is the least reactive
   - **D** it is less reactive than aluminium and copper but more reactive than iron

The structure of the Earth

The Earth

The Earth is nearly a sphere. It has a layered structure, which includes:

- a thin **crust**
- an extremely viscous (thick liquid) **mantle** that goes almost half way to the Earth's centre
- a central **core** – made of nickel and iron, the outer part is liquid and the inner part solid.

The overall density of the Earth is greater than the densities of the rocks in the crust. This means that the inside is made of a material different from the rocks of the crust. It also means that the inside of the Earth must be denser than the rocks of the crust.

Continental crustal (granitic) rocks have slightly lower densities than oceanic crustal (basaltic) rocks, which is why they project above sea level.

The crust of the Earth is moving all the time. This results in changes that include some mountains being formed and others being worn away.

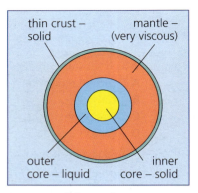

Structure of the Earth

The formation and transformation of different types of rocks can be summarised in the **rock cycle**

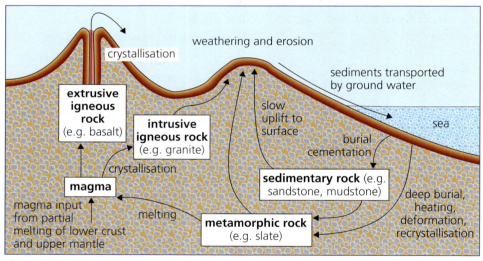

The rock cycle

Sedimentary rocks

These were formed from layers of sediment deposited on top of one another on the sea floor. The weight of sediment squeezes out the water and it becomes cemented together, with other fragments, by salts crystallising out of the water. The process often takes millions of years.

Sediments contain evidence of how they were formed. For example, if different sediments were deposited at different times the rocks will be layered; or rocks may have ripple marks that show they were formed by currents or waves.

Sedimentary rocks include **sandstone** (made of grains of sand) and **limestone** made from calcium carbonate (from shell remains of living organisms).

Sedimentary rocks usually lie on top of older rocks. These rock layers can be:

- tilted
- folded
- fractured (faulted)
- and sometimes turned upside down!

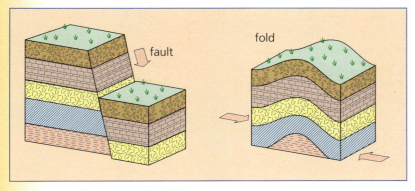

Movements of sedimentary rock

These Earth movements are caused by very large forces. Over a long time, the movements cause new mountain ranges to form (for example, the Alps are great fold mountains formed when Africa collided with Europe). New mountains replace older mountains that have been worn down (eroded) by the weather.

Metamorphic rocks

These are often found in present-day and old mountain ranges. They are formed when there is a high temperature and pressure, often caused by the mountain building process. Metamorphic rocks are igneous or sedimentary rocks that have been buried underground by Earth movements. They become compressed and heated. Their texture may change without the rock melting.

> Metamorphic rocks include **marble** (formed from limestone), **slate** (formed from shale), and **schist** (composed of interlocking crystals).

Igneous rocks

These are formed from molten rock (magma) in different ways.

- If molten rock is forced from inside the Earth up into the crust (but not onto the surface) it then cools and forms **intrusive** igneous rock (for example, granite).
- If the molten rock erupts onto the surface (for example, from a volcano) it forms **extrusive** igneous rocks (for example, basalt).

> When molten rock cools quickly it forms small crystals. When it cools slowly it forms larger crystals.

Questions

1 How do we know that the inside of the Earth must be denser than the crust?

2 Why do you think metamorphic rocks are normally associated with mountain ranges?

Earth movements

The pattern of the continents

It used to be thought that as the Earth cooled its circumference became smaller, and that this 'shrinking' forced rocks upwards to become mountains. We now know that this is not what happened.

The edges of continents are sometimes separated by thousands of kilometres of ocean. It seems that their shapes could fit together quite well (for example, South America and Africa). They also seem to have similar patterns of rocks and fossils. This suggests that they were once joined together and have moved apart over millions of years (a process known as **continental drift**).

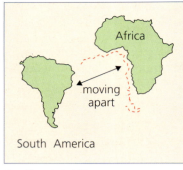

Continental drift

Tectonic plates

The Earth's **lithosphere** (the crust and upper part of the mantle) is split into a number of very large pieces – rather like a jigsaw. These pieces are called **tectonic plates**. They are moving by a few centimetres every year, because they 'float' on the underlying mantle. This is slowly moving due to convection currents created by radioactive processes deep within the Earth.

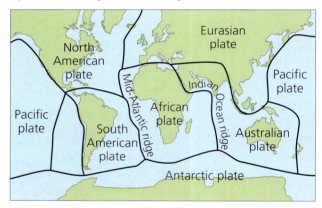

Tectonic plates

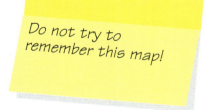

Do not try to remember this map!

Wegener first put forward these theories of continental drift caused by the movement of tectonic plates. Before that, it was thought that the major features of the Earth (for example, mountains and continents) were formed as a result of the Earth's circumference 'shrinking' when the Earth cooled down following its formation. It was not until 50 years after Wegener's death that his theories were accepted.

Earthquakes, volcanoes and ridges

Tectonic plates are always moving and this means that they are constantly pushing against each other or moving apart. Sometimes as two plates push against each other very high pressures are created. As there is such a lot of pressure, movement happens quickly. No-one can predict when earthquakes and volcanoes will happen as no-one knows when the pressure will be great enough to cause the sudden movement.

Tectonic plates may:

- slide past each other – causing an earthquake (for example, San Francisco in California)

- move towards each other – the denser oceanic plate is driven down (subducted) beneath the thicker continental plate where it melts, helping to form a layer of magma. Continental crust is forced upwards, resulting in earthquakes. The magma is under great pressure and can be forced up through the crust above to become a volcano.

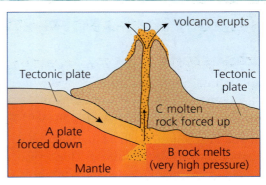

A volcano

- move apart – the crust fractures and magma rises to fill the gap resulting in a new oceanic crust. This is known as **sea-floor spreading** and is happening along oceanic ridges (for example, the mid-Atlantic ridge).

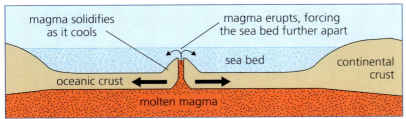

Sea-floor spreading

The Earth's polarity

As the magma spreads on the sea floor the iron-rich minerals line up in the direction of the Earth's magnetic field. The polarity or direction of the Earth's field reverses every half million years or so. The iron-rich minerals align themselves with whatever direction the field takes at the time. The magma cools to form stripes alongside the ridge. By studying the patterns of these stripes we can see how the sea floor has spread and how the Earth's magnetic field has changed over time.

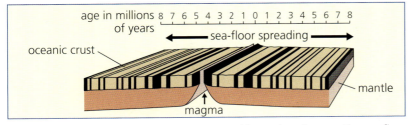

Magnetic stripes on the sea floor

Questions

1 What evidence is there that continents are moving apart?

2 In 1906 there was a disastrous earthquake in San Francisco. Recently there was a significant earthquake in Los Angeles. What do you think caused the earthquakes?

3 How do the magnetic stripes on the ocean bed provide some proof that the sea floor is spreading?

Materials from the Earth

Limestone

Limestone, a sedimentary rock, is mainly calcium carbonate. It can be quarried and used as a building material. Powdered limestone can be used to neutralise acidity in lakes and soils.

If you heat limestone in a kiln then **quicklime** (calcium oxide) and carbon dioxide are produced. This type of reaction is called **thermal decomposition**. Quicklime reacts with water to produce **slaked lime** (calcium hydroxide), which reduces soil acidity.

Cement is made by roasting powdered limestone with powdered clay. If it is mixed with water, sand and crushed rock then a slow chemical reaction produces a hard, stone-like building material called **concrete**.

Glass is made by heating a mixture of limestone, sand and soda (sodium carbonate).

Crude oil

Crude oil is obtained from the Earth's crust. It is a mixture of very many compounds.

A mixture is made up of two or more elements or compounds that are not chemically combined together. This means that mixtures can be separated by physical processes. Oil is separated by **distillation** (it is heated and then the gases that come off are condensed).

Crude oil is formed as a result of heat and pressure (over millions of years) acting on the remains of plants and animals trapped in sedimentary rocks.

Fractional distillation

Most of the compounds in oil are made from hydrogen and carbon only, and so are called **hydrocarbons**. These different hydrocarbons can be separated by evaporating the oil and allowing it to condense at different temperatures. A different 'fraction' comes off at each temperature. Each fraction consists of one type of hydrocarbon that has molecules with about the same number of carbon atoms. This is known as **fractional distillation**.

A diagram of a fractional distillation column is shown on page 55.

Hydrocarbon molecules in crude oil vary a great deal in size. The larger the molecules (which means that they have more carbon atoms) the:

- higher the boiling point of the hydrocarbon
- less volatile it is (this means it is more difficult to evaporate)
- less easily it flows (this means it is more viscous)
- less easy it is to ignite (this means it is less flammable).

This limits the use of hydrocarbons with large molecules as fuels.

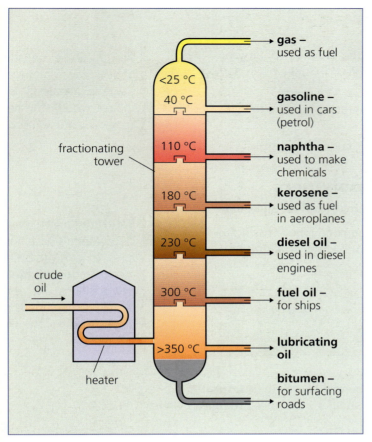

Fractional distillation

Cracking

Larger hydrocarbons can be broken down into smaller, more useful hydrocarbons by a process known as **cracking**. This involves heating the hydrocarbons to vaporise them and passing the vapours over a hot catalyst. A thermal decomposition reaction then occurs.

Some of the products of cracking are useful as fuels. Others are used to make plastics, (polymers). These are described on the next page.

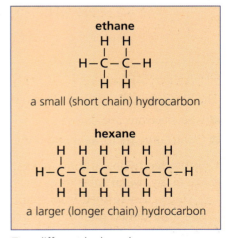

Two different hydrocarbons

Questions

1 How is slaked lime produced?

2 Why can oil be split up into different compounds using physical processes?

3 Long-chain hydrocarbons are used to put the finishing surface on roads. Short-chain hydrocarbons are used as fuels. These hydrocarbons are never used the other way round. Explain why.

Plastics

Smaller hydrocarbons produced by the 'cracking' of larger hydrocarbons from crude oil can be used to make plastics. For example:

- poly(ethene) – also known as polythene – is used to make plastic bags
- poly(propene) is used for making crates and ropes.

> Plastics can be used instead of other raw materials (for example, metals, glass, rubber, wood). This helps conserve natural resources.

Alkanes, alkenes and polymers ● ● ● ● ● ● ●

Carbon atoms form the backbone of hydrocarbon molecules.

When joined by single carbon–carbon bonds they are said to be **saturated**. These hydrocarbons are known as **alkanes**.

> **Saturated** means that the carbon atoms have no 'spare arms' to join with other atoms. In **unsaturated** hydrocarbons, one of the double carbon bonds readily breaks to join with other elements.

$$
\begin{array}{c}
\text{H} \quad \text{H} \\
| \quad | \\
\text{H}-\text{C}-\text{C}-\text{H} \qquad \text{C}_2\text{H}_6 \\
| \quad | \\
\text{H} \quad \text{H}
\end{array}
$$

Ethane – an alkane

Others have double carbon–carbon bonds. These are **unsaturated** and known as **alkenes**. Some of the smaller molecules produced by 'cracking' are alkenes.

$$
\begin{array}{c}
\text{H} \quad \text{H} \\
| \quad | \\
\text{H}-\text{C}=\text{C}-\text{H} \qquad \text{C}_2\text{H}_4
\end{array}
$$

Ethene – an alkene

The bonds are all covalent. This means that:

- the electrons are shared
- molecules are formed and not ions.

Unsaturated hydrocarbons are very reactive and can be used to make many useful substances including **polymers**. These are very large molecules formed from small molecules called **monomers**. When unsaturated monomers join together to make a polymer (with no other substances produced in the reaction) the process is known as **addition polymerisation**.

The way an addition polymer is formed can be shown like this.

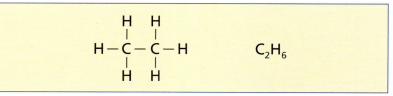

Addition polymerisation

Plastics are polymers. For example, poly(ethene) is made from ethene.

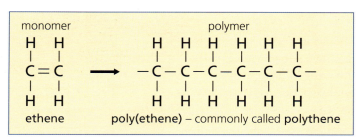

Formation of polythene

You do not need to know the polymerisation reactions for PVC and polysterene. They are shown as examples only.

Other examples of addition polymerisation include polychloroethene (known as polyvinyl chloride or PVC) and polystyrene.

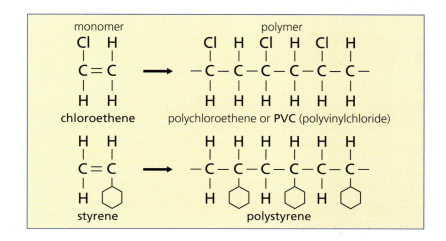

Disposing of plastics

Most plastics cannot be broken down (decomposed) by microorganisms. They are described as **non-biodegradable**. This causes problems with waste disposal.

A disadvantage of most plastics is that when thrown away as litter or in landfill sites they do not rot down like other rubbish. Litter, such as that washed up on beaches, accumulates and poses a threat to wildlife. Even when properly disposed of, plastics contain carbon 'locked up' in their molecules, so the carbon cannot be used again by plants and animals as part of the natural carbon cycle.

On the hand, many plastics are now recycled. This helps conserve natural resources and reduce the amount of waste. Also, plastics actually play a helpful role in waste disposal by providing liners for landfill sites – these prevent 'leaching' of toxic by-products of rotting waste into the surrounding land and water sources.

Questions

1 Why are unsaturated hydrocarbons so reactive?

2 Why are large hydrocarbons 'cracked'?

3 Used plastic bottles cause a litter problem. One suggestion is to burn them all. Why might this not be such a good idea?

The Earth's atmosphere

Burning fossil fuels

Burning is also known as **combustion** and is a very common type of chemical reaction. Burning produces new substances, mostly gases. When fuels burn they react with oxygen from the air. Oxidation has occurred. When a substance is burned in oxygen its elements are changed into oxides.

Most fuels contain carbon and/or hydrogen. Some also contain sulphur. The gases produced when they burn might include:

- carbon dioxide, CO_2 (from the burning of carbon)
- water vapour, H_2O (from the burning of hydrogen)
- sulphur dioxide, SO_2 (from the burning of sulphur).

Over the past 200 years, as the world has become more industrialised and energy consumption has increased, the burning of fossil fuels has resulted in a significant increase in the levels of carbon dioxide and acidic gases in the atmosphere.

Carbon dioxide causes the **Greenhouse Effect**, which scientists believe leads to global warming. Sulphur oxides and nitrogen oxides dissolve in rainwater to form **acid rain**, which kills wildlife in lakes and rivers and other enviornmental problems. (For more on these issues see the module **Environment**, pages 28 and 29.)

The atmosphere

For the last 200 million years the atmosphere has been made up of:

- about 80% nitrogen
- about 20% oxygen
- small amounts of other gases (for example, carbon dioxide, water and the 'noble' gases).

This is very different to the Earth's atmosphere 1 billion years ago, which was more like the atmosphere of Venus today. The atmosphere then was formed by a lot of volcanic activity and contained:

- water vapour
- carbon dioxide
- small amounts of methane
- small amounts of ammonia
- little or no oxygen.

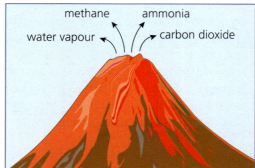

Volcanic emissions

As the Earth cooled, water vapour condensed to form the oceans.

As plants evolved, the atmosphere started to change.

- Photosynthesis led to the atmosphere gradually becoming 'polluted' with oxygen. Microorganisms intolerant of oxygen gradually died out.

- Carbon dioxide levels decreased as photosynthesising plants took up carbon dioxide, and carbon became 'locked up' in sedimentary rocks and fossil fuels.

- Methane and ammonia levels decreased as they reacted with oxygen, making it easier for new organisms to survive.

- Nitrogen gas was released into the atmosphere by dentrifying bacteria.

- Oxygen in the atmosphere led to the formation of the ozone layer, protecting life on Earth from harmful rays of the Sun.

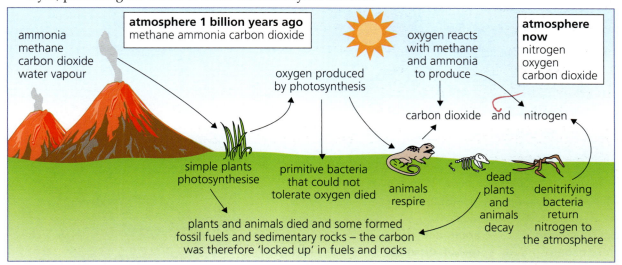

Releasing carbon dioxide

Carbonates are sometimes moved deep into the Earth as a result of geological activity. If volcanic activity breaks them down, they release carbon dioxide back into the air. In addition we burn fossil fuels, releasing carbon dioxide that has been locked up for millions of years. This fast release increases the amount of carbon dioxide in the atmosphere.

The Earth can re-absorb carbon dioxide in the oceans. Carbon dioxide reacts with sea water to produce insoluble carbonates (mainly calcium) that are deposited as sediment and soluble hydrogen carbonates (mainly calcium and magnesium), which remain in the sea. When there is too much carbon dioxide in the atmosphere this reaction increases, but even so the oceans cannot take all the increase in atmospheric carbon dioxide.

Questions

1. What were the **four** original gases in the Earth's atmosphere?
2. Explain how the amount of nitrogen gas has increased in the atmosphere over the last billion years.
3. Millions of years ago we could not have survived on Earth because of the atmosphere. Now we do survive. What changes in the atmosphere have taken place which allow us to survive?
4. Name **two** waste gases that may be released when fuels burn.

Module test questions

1 The diagram shows the rock cycle.

Match words from the list with labels 1–4 on the diagram.

metamorphic **igneous**
magma **sedimentary**

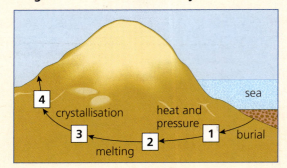

2 These sentences are about how the atmosphere changed once plants began to evolve.

Choose words from the list for each of the spaces 1–4 in the sentences.

nitrogen **ammonia**
ozone **carbon dioxide**

As a result of photosynthesis, oxygen began to pollute the atmosphere. _____**1**_____ in the atmosphere became 'locked up' in fossil fuels and sedimentary rocks. Methane and _____**2**_____ reacted with oxygen and the result of this reaction was _____**3**_____ gas. Oxygen resulted in the production of _____**4**_____, which filters harmful ultraviolet radiation from the Sun.

3 When the Earth was formed, which **two** of the following statements about the atmosphere were true?

The atmosphere contained:

A a lot of water vapour
B very little carbon dioxide
C a lot of oxygen
D no methane
E some ammonia

4 Which **two** of the following statements are true about alkanes?

A they have only short chains of carbon atoms
B they have carbon–carbon double bonds
C they have carbon–carbon single bonds
D they are more reactive than alkenes
E they are saturated hydrocarbons

5 This is a diagram of the structure of the Earth.

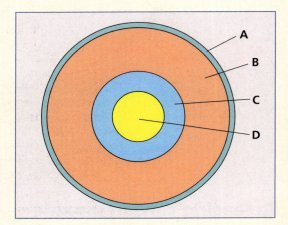

1. Which letter represents the crust?
   A B C D

2. Which letter represents the mantle?
   A B C D

3. Which letter represents the part of the Earth likely to be the most dense?
   A B C D

4. Convection currents cause the movement of the Earth's plates. Which letter represents the area where convection currents are taking place?
   A B C D

6 The first atmosphere of the Earth was a result of volcanic activity.

1. What did the volcanoes emit?
   - **A** oxygen, carbon dioxide and ammonia
   - **B** methane, ammonia and carbon dioxide
   - **C** nitrogen, methane and ammonia
   - **D** carbon dioxide, nitrogen and ammonia

2. What has reduced the amount of ammonia in the atmosphere?
   - **A** its reaction with carbon dioxide
   - **B** its reaction with methane
   - **C** its reaction with carbon dioxide and methane
   - **D** its reaction with oxygen and methane

3. What has caused the amount of nitrogen to increase?
   - **A** nitrifying bacteria
   - **B** denitrifying bacteria
   - **C** reaction of oxygen, carbon dioxide and ammonia
   - **D** reaction of carbon dioxide and ammonia

4. Two of the gases responsible for the increase in acid rain are:
   - **A** nitrogen oxides and ammonia
   - **B** sulphur dioxide and methane
   - **C** nitrogen oxides and sulphur dioxide
   - **D** carbon dioxide and ammonia

7 Crude oil is a mixture of compounds.

1. Which of the following statements is true of short-chain hydrocarbons compared to long-chain hydrocarbons?

   Short-chain hydrocarbons:
   - **A** have a higher boiling point
   - **B** are more viscous
   - **C** are more flammable
   - **D** are harder to evaporate

2. Which is the best term for the separation of the different compounds in crude oil?
   - **A** distillation
   - **B** evaporation
   - **C** fractional distillation
   - **D** condensation

3. Which of the following statements is not true about alkenes?
   - **A** they contain covalent bonds
   - **B** they have double bonds
   - **C** they easily form polymers
   - **D** they are not very reactive

4. Which of the following diagrams represents polymerisation?

A	$n\left(\begin{array}{cc} H & H \\ \vert & \vert \\ C - C \\ \vert & \vert \\ H & H \end{array}\right)$ ⟶ $\begin{array}{cc} H & H \\ \vert & \vert \\ -C - C- \\ \vert & \vert \\ H & H \end{array}_n$
B	$n\left(\begin{array}{cc} H & H \\ \vert & \vert \\ C = C \\ \vert & \vert \\ H & H \end{array}\right)$ ⟶ $\begin{array}{cc} H & H \\ \vert & \vert \\ -C = C- \\ \vert & \vert \\ H & H \end{array}_n$
C	$n\left(\begin{array}{cc} H & H \\ \vert & \vert \\ C = C \\ \vert & \vert \\ H & H \end{array}\right)$ ⟶ $\begin{array}{cc} H & H \\ \vert & \vert \\ -C - C- \\ \vert & \vert \\ H & H \end{array}_n$
D	$n\left(\begin{array}{cc} H & H \\ \vert & \vert \\ C - C \\ \vert & \vert \\ H & H \end{array}\right)$ ⟶ $\begin{array}{cc} H & H \\ \vert & \vert \\ -C = C- \\ \vert & \vert \\ H & H \end{array}_n$

Rates of reaction

If you want to increase the speed of a reaction then you could:

- increase the **temperature** – to increase the energy and frequency at which the particles bump into each other
- increase the **concentration** of the reacting chemicals – so that particles bump into each other more often
- increase the **pressure** on the reacting chemicals (if gases) – to increase the rate and frequency at which particles bump into each other
- increase the **surface area** of the chemicals (for example, chop up a solid) – so particles bump into each other more often
- use a **catalyst** – this lowers the amount of energy needed for a reaction to take place (the activation energy).

A catalyst will speed up a reaction but is not used up itself. It can be reused many times to help convert reactants into products. Different reactions need different catalysts.

How can you tell if a reaction has speeded up?

- You can measure the rate products are formed (for example, how much gas is being given off), or
- measure the rate at which the chemicals disappear (for example, a solid will get smaller).

It is possible, therefore, to compare rates of reaction. For example, when marble chips react with acid, carbon dioxide gas is given off and the solid chips get smaller. You can measure this, as shown on the graphs.

Why speed up a reaction?

In industry, speeding up a reaction will keep costs down and therefore profits up. You will make more of your product in the same time.

Many industrialised processes use biological catalysts (**enzymes**) to speed up reactions.

Using living things to do our chemistry

Chemical reactions do not just take place in big industrial areas. They are taking place inside us all the time. Our cells use chemical reactions to release energy from food and to make new materials.

We also use some microorganisms to make useful substances for us.

- **Yeast** cells convert sugar into carbon dioxide and alcohol. This is **fermentation** and is used to produce:
  alcohol for wine and beer making
  carbon dioxide – the bubbles make bread rise.
- Bacteria are used to make yoghurt from milk. They convert lactose sugar in the milk to lactic acid.

These reactions are faster when it is warm but not hot, because the catalysts for these reactions are enzymes.

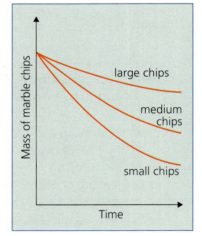

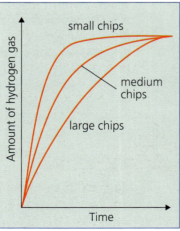

Comparing rates of reaction when marble chips are added to acid

Enzymes •

Enzymes are proteins, and so would denature (change shape) and be damaged at temperatures above about 45 °C. Different enzymes also work best at different pH values.

Enzymes can be used in everyday processes from washing clothes to making foods.

- ■ Biological detergents (washing powders) may contain protein-digesting enzymes (proteases) and fat-digesting enzymes (lipases).
- ■ These enzymes digest food stains on clothes. The clothes must be washed at a low temperature otherwise the enzymes would denature. This low temperature saves heat energy and therefore money.

A number of different foods are made by industry with the help of enzymes.

- ■ Proteins in some baby foods are pre-digested by proteases to help the baby complete the digestion.
- ■ Starch syrup can be digested into more useful sugar syrup using **carbohydrases**.
- ■ Glucose syrup can be converted into fructose syrup, which is much sweeter and therefore less needs to be used in some foods, which helps in dieting. The enzyme used in this process is an **isomerase**.

Enzymes are used in industry to bring about reactions at normal temperatures and pressure. Without enzymes, these reactions would need expensive equipment that uses a lot of energy, which adds to manufacturing costs.

Successful industrial processes depending on enzymes usually do three things.

- ■ They provide the **optimum conditions** for the organism, to make sure that it keeps producing the required enzyme for long periods.
- ■ They **immobilise** the enzyme by trapping it in an inert solid support or carrier such as alginate beads (a jelly-like substance). Immobilising an enzyme (**a**) makes it easier to recover the enzyme so it can be used again, (**b**) means that the product itself does not contain any enzyme so no expensive purification is needed, and (**c**) makes the enzyme more stable if pH or temperature changes during the process.
- ■ They allow production to carry on all the time (a **continuous process**) rather than for short periods only (**batch process**), which is more cost-effective.

The advantages of using microorganisms and enzymes to bring about chemical reactions are obvious – they enable reactions to take place more easily and this saves money.

Disadvantages are less obvious. Microorganisms and enzymes need to be tested rigorously to make sure they are safe to use, for example in foods or items that come into contact with the skin. Carrying out trials takes time and costs money, which manufacturers have to consider in their overall costings.

Questions

1. Suggest **three** ways of speeding up a chemical reaction. For each way explain why the reaction does speed up.

2. What are catalysts and why do industrial companies use them?

3. Why are enzymes so widely used in industry?

Do chemical reactions release energy?

The answer is sometimes! An **exothermic** reaction results in energy being transferred *to* the surroundings, often in the form of heat (for example, a fuel burning).

An **endothermic** reaction results in energy being taken *from* the surroundings.

During a chemical reaction:

■ energy must be supplied to break the existing bonds between the chemicals

■ energy is then released when new chemical bonds form.

In an **exothermic** reaction the energy released in forming the new bonds is *greater* than the energy used to break the original bonds – the excess energy is lost as heat. In an **endothermic** reaction the energy released in forming the new bonds is *less* than the energy used to break the original bonds – energy is therefore taken from the surroundings.

Worked example

Q Is the combustion of methane an exothermic or endothermic reaction?

A The equation for the reaction is:

methane + oxygen → carbon dioxide + water

$$CH_4 + 2O_2 \rightarrow CO_2 + 2H_2O$$

The energy needed to make or break bonds has been worked out and can be used to answer this question. These are the bonds represented in this reaction:

- methane has 4 C—H bonds
- each oxygen has 1 O=O bond
- carbon dioxide has 2 C=O bonds
- each water has 2 H—O bonds.

The energy needed to make or break each of these bonds is shown in the table.

Bonds broken:

4 C—H × 413 = 1652 kJ

2 O=O × 498 = 996 kJ

  (two molecules of oxygen)

Total = 2648 kJ energy used

Bonds made:

2 C=O × 805 = 1610 kJ

4 H—O × 464 = 1856 kJ

  (two molecules of water)

Total = 3466 kJ energy released

More energy is released than used, so the reaction is exothermic.

Bond	Energy
C—H	413 kJ
O=O	498 kJ
C=O	805 kJ
H—O	464 kJ

kJ = kilojoule which is 1000 joules

Energy is used to break bonds and energy is released when bonds are formed.

The difference between the energy used and the energy released is known as the **nett energy transfer**. If the reaction is exothermic this is negative, if it is endothermic it is positive.

A chemical reaction will take place only if the particles hit each other (collide) with enough energy. The minimum energy that is needed for a reaction to take place is called the **activation energy**.

The energy changes during a reaction can be shown by graphs.

Catalysts reduce the amount of energy required to start a reaction. They therefore reduce the activation energy.

The nett energy for the worked example is:

energy in	2648 kJ
energy out	3466 kJ
nett energy gain	−818 kJ

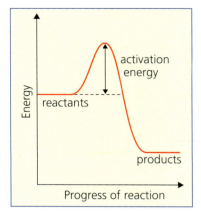

Energy changes during a reaction

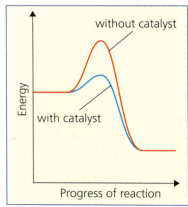

Energy changes with a catalyst

Reversible reactions

If a reaction is exothermic in one direction, it must be endothermic in the other direction. The same amount of energy will be transferred in each direction.

> **hydrated copper + (heat energy) ⇌ anhydrous copper + water**
> **sulphate (blue)   sulphate (white)**

This reaction is used the other way round as a test for water.

In reversible reactions, the products of the reaction will react to produce the substance(s) that you started with.

For example:

> **ammonium chloride ⇌ ammonia + hydrogen chloride**
> **(white solid)   (both are colourless gases)**

Questions

1 What is meant by an exothermic reaction?

2 Study the graph.
   What does the graph tell you about the reaction between nitrogen and oxygen?

3 In a reaction more energy is used in breaking the original bonds than is released in making the new bonds. Is the reaction exothermic or endothermic?

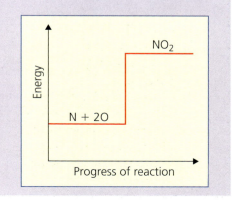

The chemistry of fertiliser production

Air is almost 80% nitrogen. It can be used to manufacture several important chemicals.

Nitrogen-based fertilisers help us to grow food. They replace the nitrogen taken from the soil by growing plants. This means that farmers can grow more – increase the yield of their crops. One problem with fertiliser is that it can run off the land and into ponds, rivers and lakes. This can contaminate our drinking water.

Ammonium nitrate fertiliser is made in the following way:

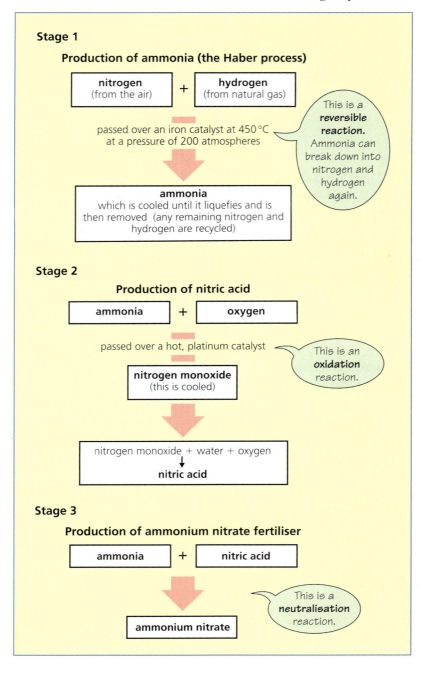

The use of fertiliser

Nitrate fertiliser is very useful as it replaces the nitrogen taken from the soil as crops grow, keeping land fertile and increasing crop yields.

However, when it gets into our drinking water it can be a health hazard, for example causing 'blue baby syndrome' in young babies. This is when the blood is not able to carry enough oxygen around the body, leading eventually to brain damage and death.

Fertilisers are therefore useful but the amounts used must be managed carefully, so that just the right amount is added to the soil to minimise run-off into rivers and lakes.

Reversible reactions and equilibrium ● ● ●

The reaction between nitrogen and hydrogen to produce ammonia is **reversible**. The reaction will go either way depending on the conditions.

reversible reaction
$$N_2 + 3H_2 \rightleftharpoons 2NH_3$$

If the reaction is going in both directions at the same rate in a **closed system**, it is said to be in **equilibrium**. A closed system is a container where no other chemicals are involved, and where none of the products are removed from the container.

Where the point of equilibrium is between the two reactions depends on the conditions. If the forward reaction is exothermic, the back reaction must be endothermic. If you add heat energy by heating the reactants, the system will shift the reaction in favour of the back reaction, which then absorbs the heat energy (you will get more reactants than products).

heat
$$N_2 + 3H_2 \rightleftharpoons 2NH_3$$

So whether there are more reactant molecules or more product molecules in the equilibrium 'mix' depends on temperature. This is an important principle behind the Haber process.

In reactions between gases, an increase in pressure will favour the reaction that produces the least number of molecules. So for this reaction, it would favour the production of ammonia.

The Haber process ● ● ● ● ● ● ● ● ● ● ● ● ● ● ● ●

The reaction between nitrogen and hydrogen in a closed system means that you could be breaking down ammonia as quickly as you were making it! This would be useless to a manufacturer.

A German scientist called Haber found that a high temperature, high pressure and a catalyst are needed to make even modest amounts of ammonia. The yield is increased if ammonia is siphoned off as it is made, and the unused reactants continually recycled so that it becomes an open system.

This graph shows the yields of ammonia in the Haber process at various temperatures and pressures. If pressures above 200 atmospheres are used the costs for equipment would increase significantly. If the reaction was allowed to run at lower temperature it would take too long. The temperature and pressure used are the most economic way to produce ammonia.

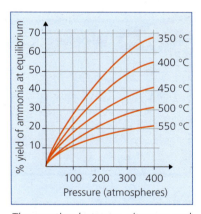

The reaction between nitrogen and hydrogen in different conditions

Questions

1   What is meant by a reversible reaction?

2   To get the maximum yield of ammonia from nitrogen and hydrogen you would need to run the reaction at 350 °C and 400 atmospheres pressure. Why do manufacturers using the Haber process not do this?

Chemical quantities

This topic is very much assessed in terms of calculations. You will, in the examination, have access to a data book. Here the information you need is printed in the table on the right.
A series of worked examples show the type of calculations you will be expected to do.

Relative formula mass of compounds

You must be able to calculate the **relative formula mass (M_r)** of a compound (given the formula).

Worked example

Q What is the relative formula mass of sulphuric acid (H_2SO_4)?

A A_r hydrogen = 2 (there are two of them)
A_r sulphur = 32
A_r oxygen = 64 (there are four of them)
M_r = 98

Relative atomic masses (A_r)	
hydrogen	1
carbon	12
oxygen	16
sulphur	32
calcium	40
iron	56

Percentage of elements in compounds

You must be able to work out the percentage of an element in a compound.

Worked example

Q What is the percentage of sulphur in sulphuric acid?

A The M_r of sulphuric acid is 98
The A_r of sulphur is 32

Therefore sulphur represents $\dfrac{32}{98}$ of the compound

This is 32.7%

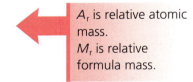

A_r is relative atomic mass.
M_r is relative formula mass.

Masses of reactants and products

You must be able to calculate the masses of reactants and products.

Worked example

On heating calcium carbonate ($CaCO_3$) it breaks down. The products of the breakdown are calcium oxide and carbon dioxide.

Q What mass of calcium oxide can be formed from 25 g of calcium carbonate?

$CaCO_3 \rightarrow CaO + CO_2$

continued ...

A From this equation:
- 1 mole of $CaCO_3$ reacts to give 1 mole of CaO and 1 mole of CO_2
  M_r calcium carbonate is 100   ($Ca = 40$, $C = 12$, $3 \times O = 48$)
  M_r calcium oxide is 56   ($Ca = 40$, $O = 16$)
  M_r carbon dioxide is 44   ($C = 12$, $2 \times O = 32$)
- Therefore 100 g of calcium carbonate will result in 56 g of calcium oxide.
- Therefore 25 g of calcium carbonate will result in 14 g of calcium oxide.

What if the product is a gas?

You must be able to calculate the volume of a reactant if it is a gas.

From the last example, the breakdown of 1 mole of calcium carbonate will result in 1 mole of carbon dioxide. Therefore 100 g of calcium carbonate will break down to produce 44 g of carbon dioxide.

However, 1 mole of *any* gas occupies 24 litres (at room temperature and pressure). So if 1 mole of calcium carbonate breaks down, then 24 litres of carbon dioxide are produced.

If 2 moles of calcium carbonate break down, then 2 moles of carbon dioxide will be produced, or $2 \times 24 = 48$ litres.

One mole is the relative formula mass of the compound in grams. Carrying out calculations in moles is simply a matter of ratios. In an exam, you may use moles but do not have to. You will be given the volume of the M_r of any gases, in litres or dm^3.

Working out chemical formulae

You must be able to determine the ratios of atoms in compounds from information you are given.

Worked example

In an investigation it is found that 5.6 g of iron react with 2.4 g of oxygen.

Q What is the formula of iron oxide?

A

	iron	oxygen
masses combining	5.6 g	2.4 g
mass of 1 mole	56 g	16 g
number of moles combining	$\dfrac{5.6}{56} = 0.1$	$\dfrac{2.4}{16} = 0.15$
the ratios are	1	to 1.5
or better still	2	to 3

The formula for iron oxide is therefore Fe_2O_3.

Questions

Use information on these pages to answer the questions.

1 What is the M_r of calcium hydroxide: $Ca(OH)_2$?

2 What is the percentage of oxygen in calcium carbonate ($CaCO_3$)?

Safety symbols

You should be able to recognise and explain what these symbols mean.

You should also be able to name one hazardous substance that is corrosive (for example, sulphuric acid).

oxidising
provide oxygen that allows other materials to burn more fiercely

harmful
similar to toxic substances but less dangerous

highly flammable
catch fire easily

corrosive
attack and destroy living tissues including eyes and skin

toxic
can cause death when swallowed or breathed in or absorbed through the skin

irritant
not corrosive but can cause reddening or blistering of the skin

Terminal exam questions

1 Ammonium nitrate is a fertiliser used by farmers. It is manufactured on a large scale in Britain.

a i Nitrogen and hydrogen are reacted together in the Haber Process. Balance the following equation.

$$N_2 + H_2 \rightarrow NH_3$$ [2]

ii State the conditions under which the two gases are reacted together. [3]

iii Explain, as fully as you can, why these conditions are used. [3]

b You will need the following information to answer this question:

Relative atomic masses (A_r)	
hydrogen	1
nitrogen	14
oxygen	16

The ammonia is reacted with nitric acid to produce ammonium nitrate.

$$NH_3 + HNO_3 \rightarrow NH_4NO_3$$

i What is the relative formula mass of ammonium nitrate? [1]

ii If 85 tonnes of ammonia are used, how many tonnes of ammonium nitrate will be produced? [4]

13 marks

2 Ethene burns in oxygen and releases carbon dioxide as a waste product. The following equation represents the reaction.

$$C_2H_4 + 3O_2 \rightarrow 2CO_2 + 2H_2O$$

In terms of the bonds, the reaction can be shown as follows:

$$\begin{array}{c} H \quad H \\ | \quad | \\ C = C \\ | \quad | \\ H \quad H \end{array} + 3\,O{=}O \rightarrow 2\,C\!\!\begin{array}{c} O \\ \diagup\diagdown \\ O \end{array} + 2\begin{array}{c} H \\ \diagdown \\ O \\ \diagup \\ H \end{array}$$

This table showing the energy required to break and make certain bonds will be helpful in answering the questions which follow.

Bond	Energy (kJ)
C—H	413
C=C	612
O=O	498
C=O	805
H—O	464

a i Work out the energy changes that take place during the reaction. [5]

ii Is the reaction exothermic or endothermic? Give a reason for your answer. [1]

b This reaction takes place very quickly. Suggest **three** ways of speeding up a reaction that takes place slowly. [3]

9 marks

3 You will need the following information to answer this question:

Relative atomic masses (A_r)	
sodium	23
chlorine	35
calcium	40

a Sodium chloride (NaCl) can be broken down to produce sodium and chlorine gas. These are two useful substances.
If 116 g of sodium chloride are broken down, what volume of chlorine gas will be released? [4]

b In an investigation it is found that 20 g of calcium reacts with 35 g of chlorine to produce calcium chloride. What is the formula of calcium chloride? [4]

8 marks

4 The diagram below shows how a beer called Newcastle Brown Ale is made.

a Use the diagram to help you to name **four** of the raw materials used to make this beer. [2]

b In the Mash Mixer sugars are formed. The reaction is helped by an enzyme. How does the enzyme help this reaction? [1]

c In the Fermenting Vessel sugars are changed into two products. One of these is alcohol (ethanol). Name the other product. [1]

d The Fermenting Vessel is cooled using cold water because the fermentation reaction gives out heat.

  i What name is given to reactions that give out heat? [1]

  ii A solution of sugar containing enzymes must not be allowed to become too hot. Explain why. [1]

e The Fermenting Vessel is kept warm to maintain a good rate of reaction. Explain, **in terms of particles**, why reactions go faster when the temperature is increased. [3]

9 marks

Total for test: 39 marks

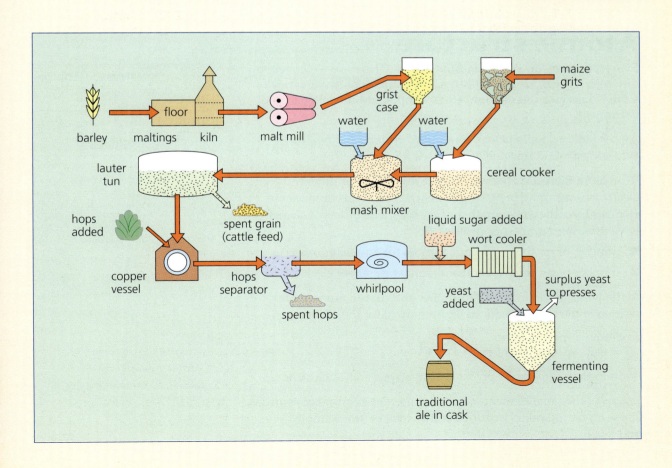

Solids, liquids and gases

When a substance gains or loses energy, it may change its state:

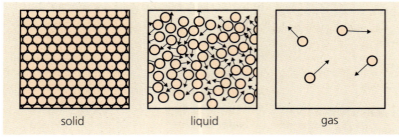

The three states of matter

If a solid is heated it gains energy and the particles vibrate more and more, until they separate and are free to move. The temperature when this happens is the **melting point**. The solid becomes a liquid.

If a liquid is heated, the particles move around more quickly. When they have enough energy to overcome the forces of attraction between them, they escape from the liquid and become a gas. This is **evaporation**.

The temperature at which a liquid boils is called the **boiling point**.

> You will already have learned about the three states of matter and what happens to particles during melting and evaporating. You need to remember this, but will not be tested on it at GCSE.

Atomic structure

Everything we know is made from **atoms**. There are well over 90 different types of atom. A substance containing only one type of atom is known as an **element** (for example, sodium, oxygen and hydrogen).

Atoms have a small nucleus containing protons and neutrons. Whizzing around this nucleus is a 'sea' of tiny electrons.

In an atom there are always the same number of protons and electrons – resulting in no overall charge. All atoms of the same element have the same number of protons. The different elements have different numbers of protons. So:

- number of protons = proton number (or atomic number)
- number of protons + neutrons = mass number

In the periodic table the mass number and proton number are written at the top and bottom of the symbol for the element.

Example: mass number 23
proton number 11 Na

Sodium therefore has 11 protons, 12 neutrons and 11 electrons.

Atoms of the same element may have different numbers of neutrons. These atoms are called **isotopes** of the element (for example, $^{35}_{17}\text{Cl}$ and $^{37}_{17}\text{Cl}$).

	Mass	Charge
proton	1	+
neutron	1	0
electron	negligible	−

Electrons

Imagine that the electrons that orbit the nucleus are in different 'shells' (like layers in an onion). The shell nearest the nucleus can hold 2 electrons. The next three shells can each hold 8 electrons. The shells are in fact **energy levels** (lowest energy nearest the nucleus). Electrons fill the lowest available energy levels, so they fill the shells closest to the nucleus. Atoms like to have full shells to make them stable. Noble gases have 8 electrons in their outer shells (helium only needs two electrons to fill its outer shell), so are very unreactive and stable.

Below are diagrams of an atom of sodium and an atom of magnesium. Sodium has 11 protons and 11 electrons. It therefore has no charge. The electronic structure of sodium can be written as 2,8,1. Magnesium has an electronic structure of 2,8,2.

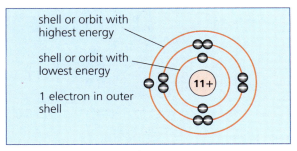

The electronic structure of a sodium atom

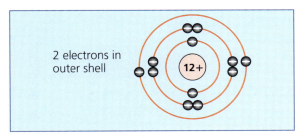

The electronic structure of a magnesium atom

You must be able to represent the atomic structure of the first twenty elements of the periodic table, using the periodic table in the data book. First you must work out the number of electrons and then place them in the shells. The first shell can take 2 electrons. The other shells take 8 electrons each. The last shell takes the number of electrons that are left.

18th century chemists knew that substances were made of different elements, but the idea that elements were made of atoms was not proved. Early in the nineteenth century John Dalton studied the way in which the different elements combine with one another to form chemical compounds. He argued that if elements were made of atoms, they would combine in definite proportions to produce particular substances. He tested this idea and was able to show that, for example, water is a compound made of two parts hydrogen to one part oxygen. He called this smallest unit of a chemical substance a 'molecule'. His measurements were the proof that chemists needed that atoms and molecules are the building blocks of all matter.

Questions

1 Chlorine (Cl) has 17 protons. What is its electronic structure?

2 How many electrons does carbon ($^{12}_{6}$C) have in its outer shell?

3 Work out the electronic structure of magnesium ($^{24}_{12}$Mg), silicon ($^{28}_{14}$Si), argon ($^{40}_{18}$Ar) and oxygen ($^{16}_{8}$O).

Compounds and chemical bonds

Ionic bonds

Most substances are compounds formed when two or more elements react and combine together. One way of forming a chemical bond is by losing or gaining an electron.

Look, for example, at the reaction between sodium and chlorine:

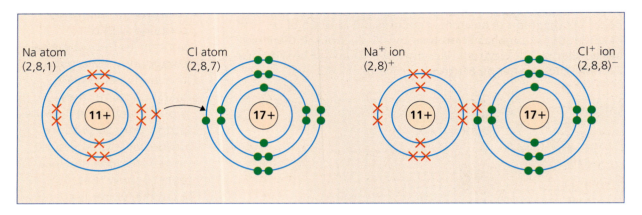

- Both elements now have a full outer shell of 8 electrons. They now have the electronic structure of noble gases.
- The sodium atom has lost one electron. It is now a positive sodium ion (it now has one more proton than it has electrons).
- The chlorine has gained one electron. It is now a negative chloride ion (it has one more electron now than it has protons).

The compound is sodium chloride (common salt). The bond between the two elements is an **ionic bond**. Ionic bonds are very strong. The compound is called an **ionic compound**.

Ionic compounds

The ions of elements in an ionic compound have opposite electrical charges and so are held together strongly by forces of electrostatic attraction. Ionic compounds form regular structures (giant ionic lattices) in which each positive ion is surrounded by negative ions and each negative ion is surrounded by positive ions. This means that the whole lattice is held together strongly.

It is not easy to break this lattice by heating because a lot of energy is needed to pull the bonds apart. So ionic compounds have high melting and boiling points.

If, however, an ionic compound is melted or dissolved in water, the ions become free to move and will conduct electricity. So, for example, solid sodium chloride (common salt) does not conduct electricity but molten sodium chloride or a salt solution will.

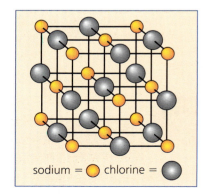

sodium = ⬤ chlorine = ⬤

The giant lattice structure of sodium chloride

Covalent bonds

Atoms can also form bonds by sharing electrons. These shared pairs are called **covalent bonds**. Atoms which share electrons often form molecules.

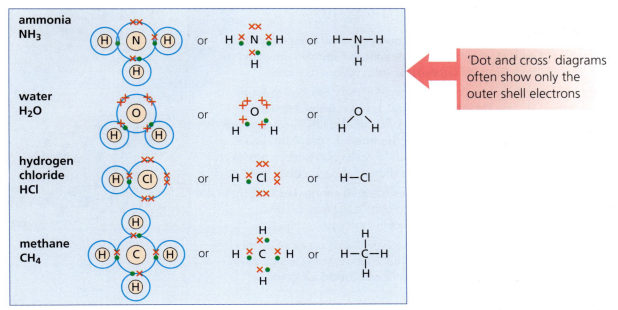

'Dot and cross' diagrams often show only the outer shell electrons

Some common covalent molecules

When they are not in compounds, all of the elements that are common gases are found in diatomic molecules. This means molecules with two atoms (for example, O_2, Cl_2).

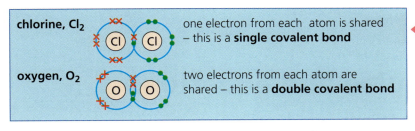

chlorine, Cl_2 one electron from each atom is shared – this is a **single covalent bond**

oxygen, O_2 two electrons from each atom are shared – this is a **double covalent bond**

Some substances can exist in covalent or ionic forms. For example:
- hydrogen chloride can be HCl molecules or H^+ and Cl^- ions
- water can be H_2O molecules or H^+ and OH^- ions

The atoms in these molecules are more stable than the atoms on their own, because their highest energy levels (outer shells) are now full. Notice how oxygen (which has six electrons in its outer shell) needs to share another *two* electrons to make it stable – so forming a **double bond**.

Questions

1. Draw a diagram to show the electronic structure of $^{40}_{20}Ca$.

2. Draw 'dot and cross' diagrams to show how you would expect calcium to react with chlorine. How many atoms of each element are involved in this reaction?

3. Carbon dioxide has the formula CO_2. Draw a diagram of the molecule to show its covalent bonds. Write down **two** other ways of showing this bonding.
   (Atomic number of C = 6, O = 8)

Covalent compounds

In compounds made of molecules there are strong covalent bonds between the atoms of the molecules but *not* between the molecules themselves. This means that the molecules can be pushed apart easily, and so substances made of molecules have low melting and boiling points.

There are one or two exceptions. Sometimes, covalent compounds take the form of giant lattices rather like ionic lattices. Examples are diamond and graphite (both forms of carbon) and silica (silicon dioxide).

Within diamond each carbon atom is covalently bonded to four other carbon atoms. This makes a rigid, giant covalent structure with high melting and boiling points. Silicon dioxide forms crystals of quartz with a 3D lattice similar to diamond. In graphite each carbon atom forms three covalent bonds with other carbon atoms and they form layers that are able to slide over each other.

In covalent compounds the molecules have no charge because they are not made up of ions. There are no 'free' electrons to move around, therefore they cannot conduct electricity.

Graphite is an exception to this because each carbon atom is only bonded to three others. This means that one electron in each atom is free to move around, and so graphite can conduct electricity.

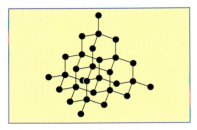
The structure of diamond

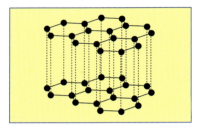
The structure of graphite

Metals

Metals consist of giant structures in which the electrons from the highest energy level (outer shell) of each atom are free to move throughout the whole giant structure. The electrons:

- hold the atoms together in a regular structure
- allow the atoms to slide over each other
- allow the metal to conduct heat and electricity.

Symbols, formulae and equations

The symbols for the elements are used to write chemical formulae for compounds. These show the ratios of atoms from the different elements that are combined to form the compound. For example, the ionic compounds calcium chloride ($CaCl_2$) and hydrochloric acid (HCl); and the covalent compounds carbon dioxide (CO_2) and ammonia (NH_3)

Equations

Equations show us what happens in a chemical reaction. The **reactants** are always on the left of the arrow. The **products** are on the right.

Reactions can be written as word equations and symbol equations. For example:

You need to remember the formulae of all common ionic and covalent compounds referred to during your GCSE course.

sodium hydroxide + hydrochloric acid → sodium chloride + water
NaOH   HCl   NaCl H_2O

The total mass of reactants is always the same as the total mass of products. This means that the same number of atoms of each element must be on each side of the arrow. The equations must be **balanced**.

For example, calcium metal and hydrochloric acid react to produce calcium chloride (a salt) and hydrogen:

$$Ca + HCl \rightarrow CaCl_2 + H_2$$

However, the number of atoms of each element must be the same on each side of the arrow. So we write:

$$Ca + 2HCl \rightarrow CaCl_2 + H_2$$

You will notice that on each side of the equation there are:

- 2 calcium atoms
- 2 chlorine atoms
- 2 hydrogen atoms.

You can also add information about the **state** of each substance in a symbol equation.

$$Ca(s) + 2HCl(l) \rightarrow CaCl_2(s) + H_2(g)$$

	State symbols
s	solid
l	liquid
aq	dissolved in water (aqueous)
g	gas

Electrolysis

During electrolysis, ions gain or lose electrons at the electrode. The atoms released at the electrodes have no charge (they are neutral). You can show this with balanced equations.

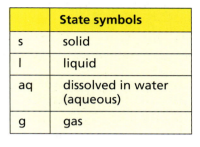

See page 81 for more about electrolysis

For example, in the electrolysis of sodium chloride:

$$2Cl^- + 2e^- \rightarrow Cl_2 \quad \text{and} \quad 2Na^- \rightarrow 2Na + 2e^-$$

Questions

1 Why are molecular substances often liquids or gases at room temperature?

2 Diamond is so hard that it is used to cut other materials. Explain this in terms of its structure.

3 Balance this equation, which represents the breakdown of hydrogen peroxide:

$$H_2O_2 \rightarrow H_2O + O_2$$

The periodic table

In the modern periodic table the elements are arranged in order of their atomic (proton) number. This means that they are also arranged in terms of their electronic structures.

From left to right, across each row (period), a particular energy level (or shell) is filled up with electrons. In the next period, the next energy level is filled up. This means that elements with similar electronic structures (that is the same number of electrons in their outer shells) are arranged in columns (Groups).

The electronic structure of elements explains the similarities and differences between their properties.

> When the periodic table was first used, scientists hadn't discovered protons so didn't know about atomic numbers. They arranged the elements in order of relative atomic mass.

The history of the periodic table

For a long time chemists searched for patterns that might explain and predict the behaviour of elements. Around 1800, John Dalton introduced the idea that chemical elements were made up of atoms, and that atoms of different elements but with similar properties could be grouped into threes or triads (for example, lithium, sodium and potassium, which are all soft reactive metals).

In 1863 Newlands introduced the idea of arranging elements in order of their atomic masses in groups of eight (octaves). A few years later Mendeléev published the first clear table, grouping elements by their atomic mass *and* properties. Not all of the elements were known at the time, so this early table had gaps. When the elements were eventually found that fitted the gaps, it strengthened the idea of the periodic table.

The classification of elements in this way led scientists to understand better why reactions take place. At first they just thought this information was interesting but not that useful. Now it is used to explain much of chemistry, and is an important summary of what we know about the structure of atoms.

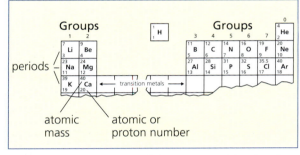

Part of the periodic table, showing the first 20 elements

Group 1 elements

These are called the alkali metals, because when they react with water an alkaline solution is produced. The alkali metals:

- are soft metals
- react with non-metals to form ionic compounds
- form ions that usually carry a +1 charge (as they lose their outer electron)

  $$2Na + Cl_2 \rightarrow 2Na^+Cl^-$$

- react with water releasing hydrogen and forming an hydroxide that dissolves in the water to form an alkaline solution

  $$2Na + H_2O \rightarrow 2Na^+OH^- + H_2$$

> A simple test for hydrogen is that it burns with a 'squeaky pop'.

When placed in cold water, alkali metals float and may well move around on the surface. The more reactive the metal, the more vigorous its reaction with water.

The further down a group the metal is, the more reactive it is and the lower its melting and boiling point. So, potassium is more reactive than sodium, which is more reactive than lithium.

These metals have different levels of reactivity, even though they all have 1 electron in the outer shell. This is because the higher the proton number (and so the number of electrons), the further the outer electron is from the nucleus. It is at a higher energy level. The further away from the nucleus, the more easily the electron is lost, and the less easily electrons are gained.

Electronic structures

lithium:	2, 1
sodium:	2, 8, 1
potassium:	2, 8, 8, 1

Non-metals

About a quarter of the elements are non-metals. They are found on the right-hand side of the periodic table.

- Group 7 and Group 0 elements have typical properties of non-metals:

- The first two Group 7 elements (fluorine and chlorine) are gases at room temperature. The third (bromine) is a liquid but vaporises at a low temperature.

- All of the Group 0 elements are gases at room temperature.

- They are brittle and crumbly when they are solid.

- Whether solid or liquid, they are poor conductors of heat and electricity (as they have no 'free' electrons in their outer shell).

Group 0 elements (noble gases)

These elements have full outer shells – that is, they do not need to gain or lose electrons in their highest energy levels. This explains why the noble gases are so unreactive, and why they exist as a single atom (unlike chlorine, Cl_2). The noble gases:

- are very stable (unreactive)

- all exist as individual atoms, not as molecules like other gases

- are used to replace air inside light bulbs (because oxygen in air *is* reactive, and would cause the filament to burn away).

Noble gases include helium, neon and argon. Helium is much less dense than air and is used in balloons.

Questions

1   You may have seen sodium and potassium react with water. Both are very reactive but potassium is noticeably more reactive than sodium. Explain this in terms of its structure.

2   Why are Group 1 metals often called 'alkali' metals?

3   Why are the noble gases so unreactive?

4   Xenon exists as atoms. Chlorine is a molecule and is diatomic. What do these statements mean?

The halogens

The halogens are the elements in Group 7 of the periodic table.

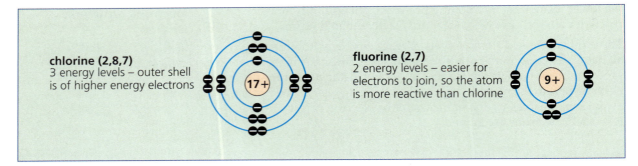

chlorine (2,8,7)
3 energy levels – outer shell is of higher energy electrons

17+

fluorine (2,7)
2 energy levels – easier for electrons to join, so the atom is more reactive than chlorine

9+

Halogens:

- have 7 electrons in the outer shell and so need gain only 1 electron to react
- if they react the halogen ion (halide) has a −1 charge
- have coloured vapours (for example, chlorine is green)
- consist of molecules that are made up of pairs of atoms (for example, chlorine Cl_2, bromine Br_2)
- form ionic salts with metals (for example, potassium chloride, calcium bromide)

The further down the group you go the:

- less reactive the gas
- higher the melting and boiling points.

Halogens are less reactive as you go down the group. This is because bigger atoms have more electrons, which occupy higher energy levels. Extra electrons need to have sufficient energy to fill the highest energy level (outer shell). This means that the atoms find it increasingly difficult to accept electrons to make ions.

The order of reactivity (from highest to lowest) is: fluorine, chlorine, bromine, iodine.

A more reactive halogen gas can displace a less reactive halogen from an aqueous solution of its salt. For example:

$$2NaI + Cl_2 \rightarrow 2NaCl + I_2$$

The chlorine is more reactive than the iodine.

Metal–halogen compounds

Sodium chloride is a metal–halogen compound. It is common salt and is found in large quantities in the sea and underground (salt mines).

It can be broken down, when in solution, by electrolysis. This is an important industrial process.

Sodium (a reactive metal) reacts with *chlorine* (a reactive non-metal and poisonous gas) to produce *sodium chloride* (common salt), which you put on your fish and chips!

Chlorine gas is formed at the positive electrode (chloride ions are negative) and hydrogen gas at the negative electrode (hydrogen ions are positive). A solution of sodium hydroxide is also formed.

There are uses for these products.

- Chlorine is used to kill bacteria in drinking water and in swimming pools.
- Chlorine is used in the manufacture of disinfectants, bleaches and in the plastic polymer PVC (polyvinyl chloride).
- Hydrogen is used in the manufacture of ammonia (the Haber process) and margarine.
- Sodium hydroxide is used in the manufacture of soap, paper and ceramics.

What happens during electrolysis?

In the electrolysis of molten sodium chloride, Cl^- ions arrive at the positive electrode. Each chloride ion loses an electron. This makes it electrically neutral – a chlorine atom again:

$$Cl^- - e^- \rightarrow Cl$$

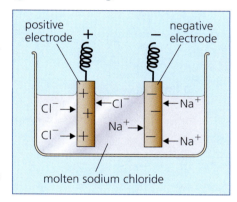

positive electrode +   negative electrode −

$Cl^- \rightarrow$ $\leftarrow Cl^-$ $\leftarrow Na^+$

$Cl^- \rightarrow$ $Na^+ \rightarrow$

$\leftarrow Na^+$

molten sodium chloride

A simple test for chlorine gas is that it bleaches damp litmus paper.

However, you need two atoms to make chlorine gas so:

$$2Cl^- - 2e^- \rightarrow Cl_2$$

More uses for the halides

Silver chloride, bromide and iodide (the silver halides) are reduced to silver by the action of light, X-rays and radiation. They are used to make photographic film and photographic paper.
Hydrogen halides (for example, hydrogen chloride) are gases that dissolve in water to produce acidic solutions.

Questions

1 The electrolysis of aqueous sodium chloride produces a number of useful substances. Draw a spider diagram that shows the substances and their uses in industry. **Useful substances from the electrolysis of aqueous sodium chloride** should be at the centre of the diagram.

2 What happens at the positive electrode during the electrolysis of molten sodium chloride?

3 Why are the halogens so reactive?

4 Give **one** example of a displacement reaction involving the halogens.

Terminal exam questions

1 a All of the elements are represented in the periodic table. Potassium is represented in this way: $^{39}_{19}K$

    i What is the atomic mass of potassium? [1]

    ii How many protons has potassium? [1]

    iii How many neutrons has potassium? [1]

b Sodium is represented in this way: $^{23}_{11}Na$
Draw a diagram to show the electronic structure of a sodium atom. [3]

c Lithium has the electronic structure 2, 1 and chlorine has the structure 2, 8, 7.

    i Draw an electronic diagram to show how the two atoms react with each other to produce lithium chloride. [3]

    ii What type of bond has been formed? [1]

    iii During this reaction the lithium atom becomes an ion. What is an ion? [2]
How does lithium become an ion? [2]

14 marks

2 a What is a molecule? [3]

b Draw a diagram of an ammonia molecule (NH_3) to show the bonds present. You should show the arrangement of the electrons. [3]

c Why do molecules generally have lower melting and boiling points than ionic compounds? [2]

8 marks

3 Group 1 metals are also known as the alkali metals. They react with water to produce metal hydroxides.

a i Balance the following equation:

    $K + H_2O \rightarrow KOH + H_2$ [1]

    ii Sodium is less reactive than potassium. Explain why. [3]

b The alkali metals react with the halogen gases to form metal halides. If sodium iodide and chlorine react together the result is sodium chloride and iodine.

    $2NaI + Cl_2 \rightarrow 2NaCl + I_2$

    Explain this reaction. [2]

6 marks

4 Sodium chloride can be broken down into sodium and chlorine gas. This is done by electrolysis.

a Why must the sodium chloride be molten before it can be electrolysed? [2]

b During the electrolysis, what would you expect to happen at the cathode? [3]

a i Give **two** uses of chlorine. [2]

    ii What is the test for chlorine gas? [3]

10 marks

5 This is a diagram of a molecule of hydrogen chloride.

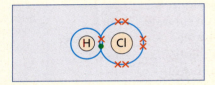

a i What does this tell you about the molecule? [3]

    ii Hydrogen is shown in the periodic table like this: ^1_1H.
What does this tell you about the structure of the hydrogen atom? [3]

b i What is meant by a diatomic molecule? [1]

    ii Use an electron diagram of an oxygen molecule to show its structure. [3]

c Molecules tend to have low melting and boiling points. Diamond is molecular but has a high melting point. Explain why. [4]

14 marks

Total for test: 52 marks

Physical processes

Energy

Electricity

Forces

Waves and radiation

Heat transfer

Conduction

Heat energy can be transferred by conduction through a substance, from a higher temperature to a lower temperature.

Metals are good conductors of heat. If a metal is heated, the ions have more kinetic energy. Free electrons transfer this heat energy to cooler parts of the metal as they move (diffuse) through it. They do this as they collide with other ions and their associated free electrons.

Non-metals are generally poor conductors (insulators). Gases are very poor conductors.

Conduction is the transfer of energy through a substance, without the substance itself moving.

Convection is the transfer of energy by the movement of liquid or gas.

Radiation is the transfer of energy to and from objects. It can take place though a vacuum.

Convection

Liquids and gases can flow, and so they can transfer heat energy from hotter to cooler areas by their own movement (convection). A good example is a heater in a room.

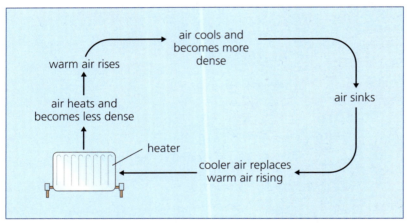

Convection

As a liquid or gas gets hotter its particles move faster. The liquid or gas expands and becomes less dense. This means that the gas will rise, or warmer liquid will rise above surrounding cooler liquid.

Radiation

Thermal radiation is the transfer of energy between objects by waves (radiation). Particles are not involved, so this transfer can happen through a vacuum.

Hot bodies (for example, the Sun) give off mainly infra red radiation. The hotter the body, the more radiation is given off.

Dark, matt surfaces emit more radiation than shiny, white surfaces (at the same temperature). Dark, matt surfaces are also good absorbers of radiation, and shiny white surfaces are good reflectors of radiation.

Houses and cars in sunny Spain are usually white to reflect heat. People in hot countries (for example, Saudi Arabia) often wear white clothing.

Energy loss from buildings •••••••••••

A lot of energy escapes from buildings in the form of heat, especially from windows and roofs. Some of the main ways in which this heat loss can be reduced include:

- double glazing – air between the two panes of glass is a very poor conductor and therefore a good insulator
- fibreglass lagging in a roof – air trapped between the fibres gives good insulation
- cavity walls – air between the bricks gives good insulation
- cavity wall insulation – air provides good insulation but if warmed it will rise and more heat lost as a result. Special foam in the cavity wall helps prevent the air rising (by convection), and so results in better insulation
- draught excluder – strips of foam around a door frame make a tight-fitting door, so warm air cannot escape.

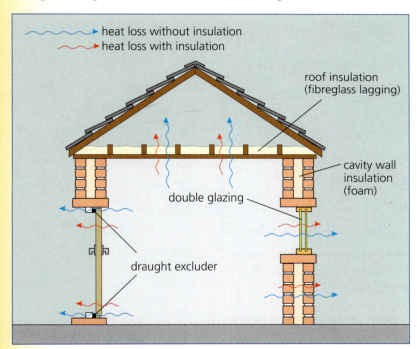

Reducing heat loss from a house

Questions

1 Why does an iron bar conduct heat so well?

2 Which type of energy transfer results in heat reaching us from the Sun?

3 A radiator is turned on in a room. You are sitting at the other side of the room. You become warmer. Explain why.

4 Cavity wall insulation is expensive. Why do some houses have it, when the air in the cavity between the bricks is a good insulator anyway?

Using electricity

Electrical appliances

An electrical appliance transfers energy from electricity to heat, light, sound or movement. The amount of electrical energy an appliance transfers depends on two factors:

- how long the appliance is switched on
- how fast the appliance transfers energy (this represents the power of the appliance).

> In an examination you may need to give examples of electrical devices and the energy transfers they bring about.

Measuring power

Energy is normally measured in joules. Power is a measure of how fast this energy is transferred. The greater the power rating of an appliance, the more energy is transferred in the same time.

$$\textbf{power} \text{ (watt, W)} = \frac{\textbf{energy transferred (joule, J)}}{\textbf{time taken (second, s)}}$$

1 watt is therefore the transfer of 1 joule of energy in one second.

Worked example

Q A light bulb transfers 1000 J of energy in 25 seconds. What is the power rating of the appliance?

A $power = \dfrac{energy\ transferred}{time}$

$power = \dfrac{1000}{25} = 40\ watts$

> In this worked example the unit for time is in seconds. Beware – in the examination it may be given in minutes.

However, the joule is a small amount of energy compared to the amounts used at home for lighting and heating. Electricity suppliers use a much bigger unit called the **kilowatt hour**. This is based on **kilowatts** which are 1000 watts.

$$\begin{array}{ccc}
\textbf{energy transferred} & = & \textbf{power} \times \textbf{time} \\
\textbf{(kilowatt hour, kWh)} & & \textbf{(kilowatt, kW)} \quad \textbf{(hour, h)}
\end{array}$$

The amount of electrical energy transferred from the mains is measured in kilowatt hours or **units**.

Worked example

Q The power of a food mixer is rated at 20 kW and is switched on for 30 minutes. How much energy is transferred?

A $energy\ transfer = 20 \times 0.5\ (half\ an\ hour) = 10\ kWh$

> In the examination you often have to convert units before carrying out the calculations

You can calculate the cost of energy, given the information:

cost of energy = number of units × cost per unit

Worked example

Q A house owner receives an electricity bill. The previous meter reading was 1487 units and this has risen to 1923. The cost per unit is 43.5p. How much is the cost of the electricity used?

A cost of energy = number of units × cost of each unit
                     = (1923 − 1487) × 43.5 = £189.66

Gravitational potential energy

Electrical energy can be transferred as gravitational potential energy (for example, a crane lifting a steel bar). This is the energy stored in an object that has been lifted against the force of gravity. The higher the object is lifted, the more energy it has.

The higher you climb, the more gravitational potential energy you have.

change in gravitational = weight × change in vertical height
potential energy (J)   (N)   (m)

Worked example

Q A crane lifts a steel bar weighing 1200 N to a height of 25 m. What is the change in gravitational potential energy of the bar?

A change = weight × change in vertical height
              = 1200 × 25 = 30 000 J

Questions

1 A heater transfers 1500 J of energy in one minute. What is the power rating of the appliance?

2 An electrical appliance has a power rating of 30 kW and is left switched on for 90 minutes. How much energy is transferred?

3 A household uses 378 units of electricity and each unit costs 45p. How much will the electricity bill be?

Energy efficiency

When energy is transferred by electricity some of it is usefully used and some of it is not. For example, when a radio is switched on the useful energy is the sound that you hear – however, some energy is wasted as heat.

All energy that is transferred (whether it was useful or 'wasted') eventually ends up in our surroundings, which then warm up. Once the energy has spread out like this it is very difficult to use again as it is difficult to trap.

That part of the energy that is usefully transferred gives us the efficiency of the appliance.

$$\text{efficiency} = \frac{\text{useful energy transferred}}{\text{total energy supplied}}$$

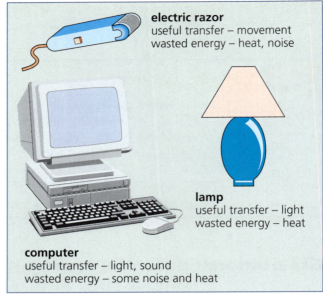

electric razor
useful transfer – movement
wasted energy – heat, noise

lamp
useful transfer – light
wasted energy – heat

computer
useful transfer – light, sound
wasted energy – some noise and heat

Energy transfers in household appliances

Worked example

Q A nightlight bulb has a power rating of 10 W and is switched on for 10 minutes. However, only 4500 J of the energy is used in a useful way. How efficient is this light bulb?

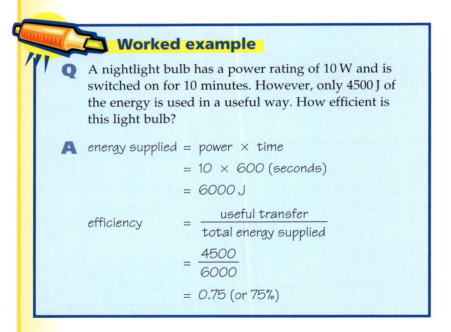

A energy supplied = power × time

= 10 × 600 (seconds)

= 6000 J

efficiency = $\dfrac{\text{useful transfer}}{\text{total energy supplied}}$

= $\dfrac{4500}{6000}$

= 0.75 (or 75%)

Earlier in this module you saw how houses could be insulated to help prevent heat loss. Some methods cost more than others, and some are more efficient. In an examination you may be asked to work out the efficiency and cost-effectiveness of the different methods. For example, you may be given the cost of each method and how much it saves on fuels bills over a year, then asked to work out the 'payback' period for each method (that is how many years it would take to recover the cost of installing that type of insulation).

For example, if cavity wall insulation costs £1000 and saves £30 per year, it would take $\dfrac{1000}{30}$ or 33.3 years to pay for itself.

Energy sources

Most power stations produce mains electricity by burning fossil fuels to heat water. Other power stations use nuclear fuels (for example, uranium and plutonium). The steam that is produced is used to drive **turbines**, which drive **generators** to make electricity.

The fossil fuels coal, oil and gas are non-renewable. It would take millions of years to replace what we have used.
Wood is a renewable fuel, because trees can be grown to replace those cut down. Other renewable energy sources include sunlight, wind, waves, running water and tides.

Fossil fuels

When fossil fuels are burned carbon dioxide is released into the atmosphere. This increases the Greenhouse Effect, which results in increased global warming.

If you compare the amounts of fossils fuels needed to produce the same amount of energy, coal releases more carbon dioxide than oil, and oil releases more carbon dioxide than natural gas. In other words, coal is the most polluting of the fossil fuels.

For more about the Greenhouse Effect and acid rain, see pages 28–29.

Most coal and oil also release sulphur dioxide, which then causes acid rain. The sulphur can be removed from the fuel or the sulphur dioxide from the waste gas, but this increases the cost of the energy produced.

Nuclear fuels

Unlike fossil fuels, nuclear fuels do not produce polluting waste gases. When running normally, very little radiation escapes into the surroundings – unless an accident occurs, when the effects could be very serious. Large amounts of dangerously radioactive material can escape and be carried great distances. Also, waste from nuclear power stations may stay dangerously radioactive for thousands of years so has to be stored very safely.

Power stations are reliable as they produce electricity at any time of day or night. However, the time it takes to start-up a power station varies a lot. Nuclear fuel takes the longest, then oil and coal. Natural gas takes the least time.

Questions

1   How do the following appliances usefully transfer energy?
    hair drier   toaster   television   vacuum cleaner

2   Which method of insulation represents the best value for money in terms of reducing heat loss?

Insulation method	Cost of installing (£)	Saving per year (£)
double glazing	2000	80
draught excluders	30	40
cavity wall insulation	1000	30
extra roof insulation	300	100

3   Describe the different risks posed by nuclear power stations and power stations using fossil fuels.

Renewable energy sources

The methods of producing electricity described on the previous page rely on fuels that will eventually run out. Electricity can also be generated from renewable sources that are 'cleaner' for the environment, but have disadvantages of their own.

Wind farms – groups of large wind generators transfer the kinetic energy of wind into electrical energy. They are usually situated on hilltops, so although they produce no chemical pollution they can be unsightly and noisy for people living nearby. It is difficult to control the supply of electricity because the amount of wind can vary.

Tidal power – rising and falling sea levels are used to power turbines to generate electricity. The supply is reliable because tides are regular, although not constant (the height the tide also varies from day to day and month to month throughout the year). There is no chemical pollution, but barrages built across estuaries can obstruct shipping and destroy wildlife habitats (for example, mud flats are home to wading birds that feed on mud-dwelling organisms).

Hydroelectric power stations transform the energy in flowing water into electrical energy. There is no chemical pollution, and the supply of electricity is reliable. Hydroelectric stations can be started quickly by allowing the water to flow. When there is excess electricity available from other sources water can even be pumped back to the top lake or reservoir. This uses electricity that would have been wasted.

However, they have to be built where there is a ready supply of running water (for example, mountains of Scotland), and this involves damming rivers and flooding land that may have been used for farming and forestry.

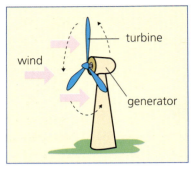

Wind power

Tidal power

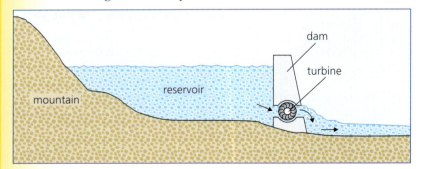

Solar cells use light energy from the Sun to produce electricity, but at a high cost. The electricity produced costs more than any other except for that stored in non-rechargeable batteries. Even so, they are often the best choice in very remote locations (for example, on satellites in space) and when you only need very small amounts of electricity (for example, watches and calculators). However, solar cells work only when sufficient light falls on them. If the sun is shining brightly they will produce a lot but on a dull day not very much. At night they produce nothing!

Geothermal energy from hot rocks below the ground can be harnessed to generate electricity. In some volcanic regions, hot water and steam rise to the surface. This can be used to turn turbines. The heat comes from rocks containing decaying radioactive elements, such as uranium. Building geothermal power stations can be expensive, but this is a reliable energy source because the hot rocks are always there and always hot.

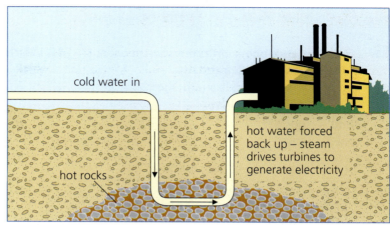

Geothermal power

Costing the Earth?

There is no single 'ideal' way of producing electricity. All the energy sources described on these pages have their advantages and disadvantages. The cleanest source might be the least reliable or too expensive to be cost-effective, or the easiest to obtain may be the most polluting.

You need to be able to identify the costs of using the various energy sources, both in terms of money and their effects on the environment. Also, you need to evaluate these costs against the benefits to society.

Here are some more points to think about:
- Renewables may have no fuel costs and be better for the environment, but the energy contained in moving water, wind, sunshine and hot rocks is more 'dilute' than in fuels, and so the cost of the equipment to harness that energy is high.
- Fuel costs for nuclear power are low, but the building and decommissioning costs of nuclear power stations are very high.
- Demands for electricity need to be matched by the ability to supply it – some sources are not reliable enough for customers needing a constant supply of electricity.

Questions

1. Copy and complete the table to show one advantage and one disadvantage of each type of energy source.

2. Which of the sources of energy in question **1** are renewable energy sources?

3. Suggest, with reasons, suitable areas to build wind farms.

Energy source	Advantage	Disadvantage
coal		
hydroelectric		
nuclear		
wind turbine		
tidal		

Module test questions

1 This question is about different sources used in the generation of electricity.

Match words from the list with each of the numbers 1–4 in the table.

wind   **nuclear**
coal   **solar**

	Information about the source
1	there is no air pollution but cloud cover reduces the amount of electricity generated
2	there is little, if any, air pollution in normal circumstances but the costs of closing down are high
3	there is no air pollution but areas of natural beauty can be affected
4	there is air pollution and the resource will run out in the not too distant future

2 This question is about units.

Match words from the list with numbers 1–4 in the table.

watt   **joule**
newton   **metre**

	The unit is relative to
1	calculations involving energy
2	changes in vertical height
3	calculations involving weight
4	calculations involving power

3 These sentences are about energy transfer. Match words from the list to the spaces 1–4 in the sentences.

vacuum   **radiation**
waves   **conduction**

In ____1____ the energy transfer is by ____2____ and the transfer can take place through a ____3____. In ____4____ the energy is transferred from a hotter part of a substance to a cooler part.

4 Which **two** statements about cavity wall insulation are correct?

A radiation of heat is prevented by the foam in the cavity wall

B air is a good insulator and so helps to prevent heat loss

C air conducts heat quite well but the foam prevents it

D the foam completely fills the space forcing the air out

E the foam prevents convection of the air in the wall

5 Which **two** of the following statements about convection are correct?

A as a gas or liquid heats it becomes less dense

B as a gas or liquid heats the particles move closer together

C the particles within the gas or liquid transfer the energy as heat

D as a gas rises it cools down

E the energy transfer is able to take place through space

6 These are diagrams illustrating four ways of generating electricity.

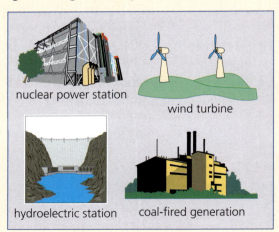

nuclear power station

wind turbine

hydroelectric station   coal-fired generation

1. In electricity generation, what is the function of steam?

A to lubricate the machinery

B to drive the turbines

C to dissolve impurities made in the process

D to drive the generators

2. Which of these methods of generating electricity is the most expensive to close down safely (decommission)?

    A wind generators
    B hydroelectric power stations
    C nuclear power stations
    D coal-fired power stations

3. Which of these pairs of methods of electricity generation do not rely on the production of steam?

    A nuclear and coal
    B hydroelectric and wind
    C hydroelectric and nuclear
    D wind and nuclear

4. Which **one** of the following pairs of methods of electricity generation is generally agreed to be the 'cleanest' for the environment?

    A hydroelectric and wind
    B nuclear and wind
    C hydroelectric and nuclear
    D wind and coal

7 This question is about the transfer of energy as heat. This is a diagram of a cup of tea cooling down.

1. How is heat energy being lost at point X?

    A convection into the wooden bench
    B radiation into the wooden bench
    C convection through the cup followed by radiation into the bench
    D conduction into the wooden bench

2. How is heat energy being lost at point Y?

    A convection of the air
    B conduction into the air
    C radiation followed by conduction
    D convection followed by radiation

3. Which type of surface would result in the cup radiating more heat energy?

    A dark and shiny
    B bright and shiny
    C dark and matt
    D bright and matt

4. Which sentence best describes radiation?

    A the transfer of heat energy through a solid
    B the movement of air
    C the transfer of heat between two substances touching each other
    D the transfer of heat by waves

8 This toaster has a rating of 840 W.

1. If it is switched on for 1 minute, how much energy does it transfer?

    A 840 J
    B 50 400 J
    C 7 J
    D 8400 J

2. If the toaster is used for 20 minutes, how much energy will have been transferred in terms of kilowatt hours?

    energy transferred = power × time
    (kWh)   (kW)   (h)

    A 16 800 kWh
    B 280 kWh
    C 0.28 kWh
    D 42 kWh

3. Which of the following is useful energy transferred by the toaster?

    A heat
    B noise
    C movement
    D light

4. You can heat food by placing a saucepan on top of the hot plate of a cooker. What type of energy transfer is mainly responsible for heating the food?

    A convection
    B radiation
    C waves
    D conduction

...suring electricity

An electrical current is a flow of **charge**. It is transferring energy in the form of electricity from the mains or battery to an appliance. If this current has to pass through something that offers **resistance** (a **resistor**) the energy is converted to heat. In light bulbs this heat also provides light.

The rate of energy transfer · · · · · · · · · · ·

By measuring the current and the potential difference in a circuit, you can work out the rate of energy transfer, or the **power**, of a circuit.

The speed at which energy is transferred in a circuit is measured in watts (or kilowatts).

> **power** (watts) = **potential difference** (volts) × **current** (amps)

The amount of energy transferred

How can we calculate how many joules of energy are transferred? Our equipment measures volts and amps, not joules. This formula helps us part of the way:

> **energy** (joules) = **potential difference** (volts) × **charge** (coulombs)

A coulomb is the unit of charge. One coulomb equals one ampere passing through in one second, so:

> **charge** (coulombs) = **current** (amperes) × **time** (seconds)

You can now use the reading from your ammeter to find the charge in a circuit and combine this with your readings from your voltmeter to find the amount of energy transferred.

Potential difference is the difference in energy between two points in a circuit. It is measured in volts, and so is also called **voltage**.

Potential difference across a component is measured using a **voltmeter** connected in parallel with the component.

The current flowing through a circuit is measured in amperes (A) using an **ammeter** connected in series with the component.

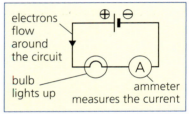

electrons flow around the circuit

bulb lights up

ammeter measures the current

An ammeter is connected in series

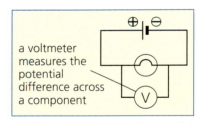

a voltmeter measures the potential difference across a component

A voltmeter is connected in parallel

Worked example

Note: at the highest examination levels you have to use the results of using one formula to work out the final answer using a second formula.

Q A current of 15 A flows through an appliance for 2 minutes. The voltage supplied to the appliance is 230 V. How much energy has been transferred?

A energy transferred = potential difference × charge.

We only know the potential difference but we can work out the charge from:

charge = current × time

= 15 × 120 (time is in seconds) = 1800 coulombs

energy transferred = p.d. × charge

= 230 × 1800 = 414 000 J

Circuits

In circuits with the components connected in **series**:

■ the total resistance is the sum of the resistances of the individual components

■ the same current flows through each component (as the current has no alternative but to flow through all of the components)

■ the total potential difference of the supply is shared between all of the components.

In circuits with the components connected in **parallel**:

■ there is the same potential difference (p.d.) across each component

■ the current through each component depends on the resistance of the component – the greater the resistance, the smaller the current (this is because in a parallel circuit the current can flow around the circuit of least resistance)

■ the total current through the whole circuit is the sum of the current running through the individual parts.

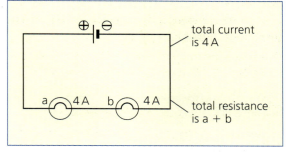

A series circuit with two lamps

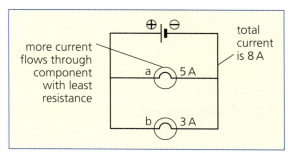

A parallel circuit with two lamps

Power is supplied to a circuit by cells. The potential difference provided by each of the cells connected in series must be added together to find the total potential difference supplied by the cells.

Several *cells* connected in series are called a *battery*.

You must know these **circuit symbols** for the examination:

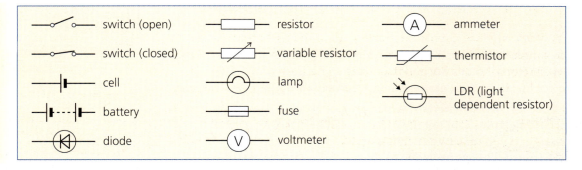

Questions

1 Power can be expressed as the amount of energy transferred in one second:

$$\text{power (watts)} = \frac{\text{energy transferred (joules)}}{\text{time (seconds)}}$$

Use this formula for finding the amount of energy transferred, to show how power can be calculated by the formula:

power (watts) = **potential difference** (volts) × **current** (amps)

2 You turn on the light switch in your bedroom. Why does the bulb give out light?

Resistance

This is the measure of how difficult it is for the current to flow. The bigger the resistance, the smaller the current produced by a particular voltage.

The relationship between resistance, current and potential difference is shown by this formula:

potential difference	**=**	**current**	**×**	**resistance**
(volt, V)		(ampere, A)		(ohm, Ω)

Current-voltage graphs are used to show how the current flowing through a component varies with the voltage across the component. So the gradient of the graph shows how much resistance the component presents.

These current-voltage graphs show the effect of sending the voltage in either direction through the component:

- The current through a resistor is proportional to the voltage across the resistor at the same temperature. This means that as the voltage increases, the current increases at the same rate.
- The resistance of a filament lamp increases as the temperature of the filament increases.
- The current through a diode flows in one direction only – it has a very high resistance to current trying to flow the wrong way.

The resistance of a light-dependent resistor decreases as the light intensity increases (for example, a burglar alarm).

The resistance of a thermistor decreases as the temperature increases (for example, a thermostat).

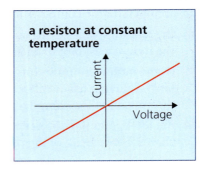

a resistor at constant temperature

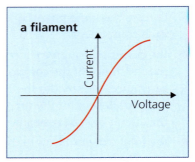

a filament

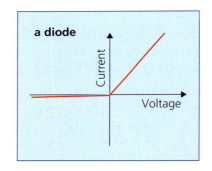

a diode

Static electricity

In solid conductors, like copper wires, the electric current is a flow of electrons. Metals are good conductors because some of the electrons from their atoms can move freely through their structure.

However, many materials, which are not good conductors (through which electrons will not flow freely), can build up an electrical charge. If you take two such materials and rub them together, electrons will pass from one to the other. The materials losing electrons become positively charged. The material gaining electrons becomes negatively charged. This is **static electricity** and the materials are **electrostatically charged**.

Static electricity can be generated by rubbing strips of clear plastic and polythene on a dry woollen cloth. The polythene gains electrons and becomes negatively charged. The plastic strips lose electrons and become positively charged.

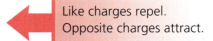

Like charges repel.
Opposite charges attract.

The greater the charge that an object picks up, the greater the potential difference (measured in volts) between the object and the Earth. If this voltage becomes large enough a spark will jump across the gap from the object to any earthed conductor. Lightning is the most dramatic example of this.

Making use of static electricity

Electrostatic charges are used in everyday appliances. This is what happens in a **photocopier**:

1. A copying plate is electronically charged.
2. The image of what you want to copy is projected on to the plate.
3. Where light from the copier bulb falls on the plate, the charges leak away.
4. The parts of the plate that still have a charge attract the black powder.
5. This powder is transferred from the plate to a sheet of photocopy paper.
6. The paper is heated and the powder sticks.
7. You now have your photocopy!

This is what happens in an **electrostatic smoke preciptator**:

Burning fossil fuels in power stations pollutes the atmosphere. Smoke is part of the pollution produced. Smoke is tiny particles of solid matter. It is removed by using the principles of electrostatics using a smoke precipitator.

1 On the way up the chimney the smoke in the waste gases passes through a negatively charged grid.
3 The smoke particles become negatively charged and are therefore repelled by the grid.
3 They are attracted by the positively charged collecting plates lining the chimney walls.
4 These positively charged metal plates are attached to Earth.
5 The smoke particles now lose their charge and drop to the bottom where they are collected.

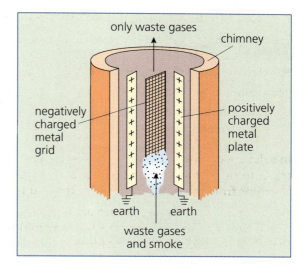

Questions

1 Study the current-voltage graphs on the facing page. Describe what each graph tells you about how the current varies with the voltage through the **three** different components.

2 What causes charge on the photocopier plate to leak away, and what does this result in?

Electromagnets

If an electric current flows through a coil of wire it causes the wire to behave like a magnet. One end becomes a north-seeking pole and the other end a south-seeking pole. This is an **electromagnet**. It can be switched on and off by turning the current on and off. If the current is reversed, the poles are reversed also.

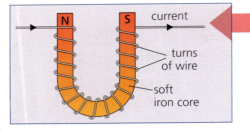

A simple electromagnet

A **bar magnet** has a north pole and a south pole. Opposite poles attract. Like poles repel.

A magnet exerts a force on any piece of magnetic material (for example, iron and steel), or another magnet, placed near to it. There is a **magnetic field** around the magnet.

If you place a wire in a magnetic field it experiences a force. The size of this force can be increased by:

- increasing the strength of the magnetic field
- increasing the size of the current flowing through the wire.

If the direction of the field or the current is reversed, the wire experiences an opposite force.

A whole range of electrical appliances and components (that is, those with electric motors) are based on wires acting like magnets when electric currents flow through them.

The d.c. motor

An electromagnet is used to turn a coil.

This is how it works:

- The battery is turned on. The current flows.
- The coil turns due to the force fields from the magnets at either side.
- When the coil is vertical the forces are equal, but the momentum of the coil carries it over.
- The split ring keeps switching the direction of the current so that it flows first one way and then the other, and the coil keeps spinning.

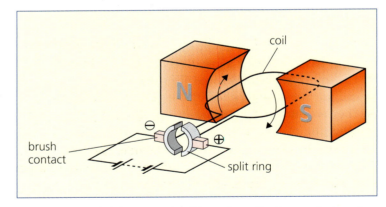

You do not need to know in detail how the split ring works in a d.c. motor.

Mains electricity

Direct current (d.c.), like that supplied to the d.c. motor described above, flows in the same direction all the time. This is the type of current supplied by cells and batteries.

Mains electricity, however, has an alternating current (a.c.). This means that the current is constantly changing direction. It does so with a frequency of 50 cycles per second (50 hertz, Hz). This means it changes direction and back again 50 times each second.

You can see the difference between a.c. and d.c. on an oscilloscope. This tells you the frequencies and peak voltages of the electricity supplied.

In the UK, mains electricity is supplied at 230 V. If not used safely, it can kill.

Electrical safety

Most electrical appliances are connected to the mains using a cable and a 3-pin plug.

Cable is made of two or three inner cores of copper wire (because copper is a good conductor). These are surrounded by a protective coat of flexible plastic (a good insulator).

Plugs have a plastic or rubber case (good insulators), brass pins (good conductor), a cable grip (to hold the wires firmly) and a fuse.

- The brown **live** wire is very dangerous. It connects to the live terminal of the mains supply. It carries a high voltage that alternates between positive and negative with respect to the neutral wire.

- The **blue** wire connects to the neutral mains terminal. It stays at a voltage close to zero with respect to the earth.

- The **green/yellow** wire connects the metal casing of an appliance with the 'earth' pin in the plug. This gives the current in an appliance a safe route down to the earth should the brown 'live' wire accidentally touch the metal casing. If an appliance is not earthed, you could get an electric shock when you touch it.

The diagram shows a correctly wired plug. In an examination you may be given a diagram of an incorrectly wired plug and be asked to 'spot the difference'.

Fuses protect electrical appliances. If a fault causes an increased current to flow, the fuse becomes hot and breaks. This breaks the circuit and switches off the current. The fuse in a plug should always be the same as the one recommended by the manufacturer. This will have a fuse rating just a little higher than the current normally flowing through the appliance.

Circuit breakers are a safer alternative to fuses. They contain an electromagnet. When the current becomes high enough then the strength of the electromagnet increases sufficiently to separate a pair of contacts. This breaks the circuit. Circuit breakers work more quickly than a fuse and are easy to reset by pressing a button.

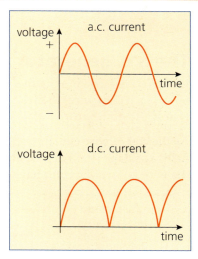

Oscilloscope traces

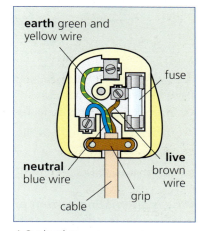

A 3-pin plug

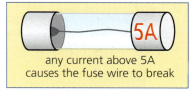

any current above 5A causes the fuse wire to break

A 5A fuse

Questions

1 What is meant by an alternating current?

2 Suggest **two** ways in which circuit breakers are better than fuses.

Making and supplying electricity

The a.c. generator

If you rotate a coil of wire in a magnetic field (or rotate magnets around a coil of wire) then you will induce an electric current. This is how the **generator** works.

As the coil of wire cuts through the lines of force of the magnetic field, a voltage (p.d.) is produced between the ends of the wire. If the wire is part of a complete circuit then a current will flow.

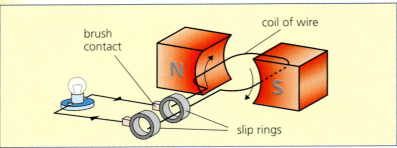

The generator
Spinning movement within magnetic field = electrical current

The motor
Electrical current within magnetic field = spinning movement

You can increase the size of the voltage by doing any, or all, of the following things:

- move the coil of wire faster
- increase the strength of the magnetic field
- increase the number of turns on the coil
- increase the area of the coil.

Why is alternating current produced?

As the coil spins, the poles will keep reversing relative to the coil. Each time they reverse, the current will flow in the opposite direction through the coil.

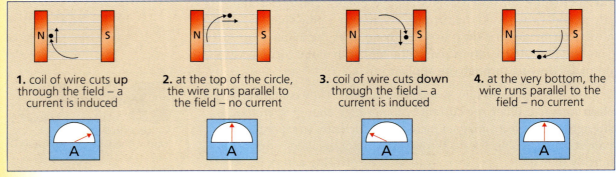

1. coil of wire cuts **up** through the field – a current is induced

2. at the top of the circle, the wire runs parallel to the field – no current

3. coil of wire cuts **down** through the field – a current is induced

4. at the very bottom, the wire runs parallel to the field – no current

Alternating current

What are the slip rings used for?

The current has to be taken away from the generator. With the coil spinning, ordinary wires would twist and break. Two continuous slip rings are used to prevent the wires twisting and to ensure that the current is a.c. (Brush contacts are used to transfer current to and from the slip rings.)

This is the principle behind electricity generating power stations. Steam is used to drive turbines, which in turn drive the generators. The generators then produce electricity.

Using tidal power or hydroelectric power, it is water that drives the turbines. Steam does not need to be produced by burning fuels. These are, therefore, environmentally more 'friendly'.

Transformers

These are used at power stations to produce very high voltages for transmission through power lines. Transformers near houses then reduce this voltage so that it is useable with household appliances.

The higher the voltage transmitted in our power lines, the smaller the current needed to transmit electricity at the same rate. A high current would heat up the power lines, resulting in a waste of energy.

How does a transformer work?

A transformer consists of two separate coils wound around an iron core. When an alternating voltage is supplied to one coil (the primary coil) it induces (causes) an alternating voltage in the other coil. The calculations are simply a matter of using ratios. The formula is:

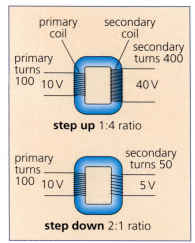

The transformer

$$\frac{\text{voltage across primary coil}}{\text{voltage across secondary coil}} = \frac{\text{number of turns on primary coil}}{\text{number of turns on secondary coil}}$$

Worked example

Q 200 V is supplied to the primary coil in a transformer. This coil has 50 turns. The secondary coil has 200 turns. What voltage is induced in the secondary coil?

A In terms of ratios, the secondary coil has 4 times as many turns as the primary coil. This means the induced voltage will be 4 times as great (4 × 200 V), which is 800 V.

Using the formula:

$$\frac{\text{voltage across primary}}{\text{voltage across secondary}} = \frac{\text{number of turns on primary}}{\text{number of turns on secondary}}$$

$$\frac{200}{x} = \frac{50}{200} \quad \text{or} \quad \frac{1}{4}$$

$$x = 4 \times 200 \quad \text{or} \quad 800 \text{ V}$$

Questions

1 A transformer is supplied with 200 V. The primary coil has 50 turns and the secondary coil has 2500 turns. What is the voltage induced?

2 You supply a transformer with 5000 V but you want to step the voltage down to 200 V. What must you make the ratio of primary to secondary turns on the coils?

Module test questions

1 These diagrams show some components that may be found as part of an electrical circuit.

Choose words from the list for each of the components 1–4 in the drawings.

resistor
diode
fuse
thermistor

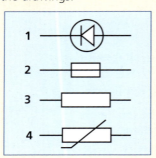

2 The table gives information about how current flows through various electrical components.

Match words from the list with each of the numbers 1–4 in the table.

thermistor   **diode**
LDR   **resistor**

	How the current flows
1	current flows in one direction only
2	the resistance decreases as light intensity increases
3	the resistance decreases as the temperature increases
4	the current is proportional to the voltage at the same temperature

(LDR = light dependent resistor)

3 These sentences are about how a d.c. motor works.

Choose words from the list for each of the spaces 1–4 in the sentences.

force field   **battery**
current   **split ring**

When the _____**1**_____ is turned on a current flows. The coil turns because of the _____**2**_____ . When the coil is vertical momentum carries the coil over. Because of the _____**3**_____ the _____**4**_____ now flows the other way and the coil keeps spinning.

4 Which **two** of these statements are true of the graph showing current against voltage?

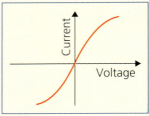

A there is no current if the voltage is reversed

B as the voltage increases so does the current, but eventually the current increases more slowly

C the current is directly proportional to the voltage

D as the voltage is reversed the current still increases as the voltage increases

E the current is inversely proportional to the voltage

5 You can increase the strength of an electromagnet by doing which **two** of the following things?

A increasing the current

B making the turns on the coil larger

C increasing the number of turns on the coil

D increasing the resistance of the wire

E moving an iron core out of the coil

6 This is a diagram of an a.c. generator.

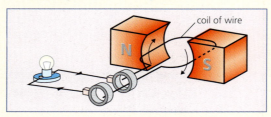

coil of wire

1. What happens when the coil spins?

A a voltage is induced

B the resistance of the coil increases

C a current is induced

D the coil sets up its own magnetic field

2. Which of the following would not increase the voltage?

A increasing the strength of the magnetic field

B decreasing the area of the coil

C moving the wire faster

D increasing the number of turns on the coil

3. In which of the following forms of power generation is water not turned into steam?

    A coal-fired   **B** nuclear

    C gas-fired   **D** hydroelectric

4. Why are transformers used at power stations?

    A to decrease the resistance of power lines

    B to alter the voltage

    C to allow a greater current to flow

    D to increase the temperature at which the wires transmit the electricity

7 The graphs show how current (I) varies with voltage (V) for three different components.

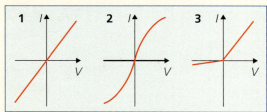

1. The best description of how current varies with voltage in graph 1 is:

    A as voltage increases so does current, but it will only flow in one direction

    B as the voltage increases the current decreases

    C as the current increases the voltage decreases

    D as the voltage increases the current increases

2. The best description of how current varies with voltage in graph 2 is:

    A voltage and current are directly proportional to each other

    B as the voltage increases so does the current, but at a certain point the current increases less

    C current increases with the voltage but the current will only flow in one direction

    D as the current increases so does the voltage, but at a certain point the voltage increases less

3. The best description of how current varies with voltage in graph 3 is:

    A as the voltage increases so does the current, but the component will only allow the current to flow in one direction

    B the current will flow in both directions but the voltage will not

    C as the current increases so does the voltage and the current will flow in both directions

    D the current and voltage are always directly proportional to each other

4. Which of these is likely to be the component in graph 3?

    A resistor

    B filament

    C variable resistor

    D diode

8 This is a diagram of a d.c. motor

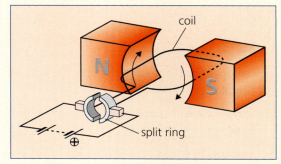

1. What causes the coil to pass the vertical position?

    A it is attracted by the South pole

    B it is repelled by the North pole

    C the momentum of the coil

    D the voltage in the wire

2. The function of the split ring is to:

    A maintain current flowing in the same direction

    B increase the current

    C switch the direction of the current

    D increase the voltage

3. An a.c. generator produces alternating current. What is the frequency of alternating current measured in?

    A hertz   **B** ohms

    C watts   **D** coulombs

4. A supply of 250 V reaches the primary coil of a transformer. The primary coil has 50 turns. You would like a voltage of 50 V from the secondary coil. How many turns should there be in the secondary coil?

    A 300   **B** 12 500

    C 200   **D** 10

Speed, velocity and acceleration

Distance-time graphs

The **speed** of an object moving in a straight line and at a steady speed can be calculated using this formula:

$$\text{speed (m/s)} = \frac{\text{distance travelled (m)}}{\text{time (s)}}$$

If an object moves in a straight line, the distance it has gone (from a certain point) can be shown by a distance-time graph.

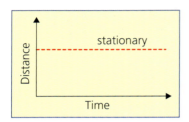

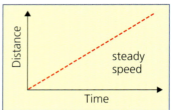

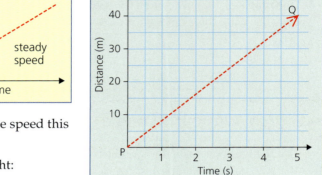

The steeper the slope of the graph, the greater the speed this represents.

So, for the distance-time graph shown on the right:

$$\text{speed} = \frac{40\,\text{m}}{5\,\text{s}} = 8\,\text{m/s}$$

You must be able to calculate the gradient of a distance-time graph.

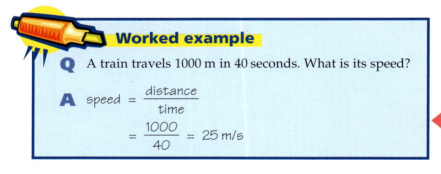

Worked example

Q A train travels 1000 m in 40 seconds. What is its speed?

A $speed = \dfrac{distance}{time}$

$\qquad = \dfrac{1000}{40} = 25\,m/s$

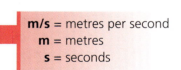

m/s = metres per second
m = metres
s = seconds

Velocity-time graphs

Velocity is the speed of an object in a straight line and in a given direction.

Velocity-time graphs represent the movement of an object travelling at a constant velocity or at a constant acceleration.

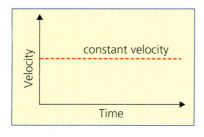

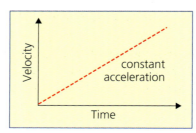

The **acceleration** of an object is the rate at which its velocity changes. For an object moving in a straight line with steady acceleration, its acceleration can be calculated by taking the change in its velocity between one point and another, and then dividing this by the time taken to get from the first point to the second.

$$\text{acceleration (m/s}^2) = \frac{\text{change in velocity (m/s)}}{\text{time taken for the change (s)}}$$

You must be able to calculate:

- the gradient of a velocity-time graph (and interpret this as acceleration)

- the area under a velocity-time graph for an object moving with constant acceleration (and interpret this as distance travelled).

> Always remember to include units unless they are given. Examiners may use km or other units – don't be tricked

Worked example

Q An aeroplane accelerates towards take-off. The graph shows how its velocity changes in the first four seconds.

    a What is the acceleration of the aeroplane?
    b What distance does it travel in this time?

A **a** $\text{acceleration} = \dfrac{\text{change in velocity}}{\text{time}}$

$$= \frac{20}{4} = 5 \text{ m/s}^2$$

    (always remember the units)

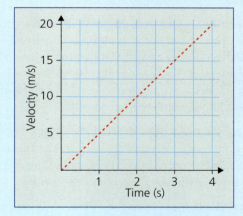

b The area of the graph is
  80 (4 × 20)

The area under the velocity-time line is
40 (0.5 × 4 × 20)

So the distance travelled is 40 m.

Questions

1 A car travels 60 m in the first 4 seconds of its journey. Calculate its average velocity and acceleration.

2 You get on your bike to go to the local shop. You accelerate until you reach a constant speed. As you get closer to the shop you slow down, before stopping very suddenly as you press the brakes too hard. Draw a very simple graph to illustrate this.

3 How is velocity different to speed?

Speeding up and slowing down

Balanced forces

Wherever two objects interact they exert a force on each other. If the forces are equal and opposite they cancel each other out – they are **balanced forces**. This means that if the object is still to start with, it will not move.

If an object is moving and the forces on it are balanced, it will carry on moving at the same speed. When a car is travelling at an unchanging speed the forces are balanced – the force from the engine is the same as the force opposing it.

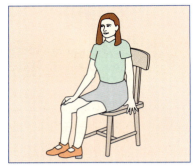
Balanced forces

Unbalanced forces

If the forces are not balanced, a stationary object will move. The forces are said to be **unbalanced**. In the example on the right, if the force exerted downwards by the person is more than the force exerted upwards by the chair, then the person will crash through the chair!

A stationary object always moves in the direction of the unbalanced force. If an object is already moving in the direction of an unbalanced force, it will speed up (accelerate). The greater the force, the greater the acceleration. So, the more force an engine can apply to a car, the faster it will accelerate.

Unbalanced forces

Also, the bigger the mass of the object, the greater the force needed to give that object a particular acceleration. For example, a heavy car needs a more powerful engine than a lighter car to get from 0 to 60 mph in the same number of seconds.

Any object moving in the opposite direction to an unbalanced force will slow down. The greater the force, the more it slows down. If a large, heavy boulder is rolling towards you, you need to push harder to stop it than you would a small, light boulder.

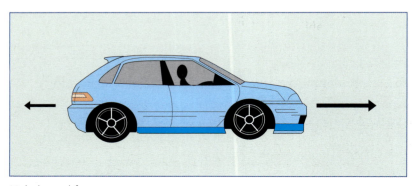
Unbalanced forces

Downwards acceleration

Objects moving downwards are accelerated by the force of gravity. On Earth the gravitational field strength is about 10 N/kg. Your weight is actually your mass in kilograms multiplied by the force of gravity.

weight = mass × gravitational field strength
  (N)   (kg)   (N/kg)

Worked example

Q A person on the Earth has a mass of 70 kg. What is that person's weight?

A weight = mass × force of gravity
= 70 × 10
= 700 N (remember the units)

Weight is often wrongly expressed in kilograms – bathroom and kitchen scales show kilograms. This is actually your mass. Your weight should be expressed in newtons.

Transferring energy

An object moves when work is done – when energy is transferred. The amount of work (in joules) done can be related to movement (in metres) by this formula:

work done = force applied × distance moved in direction of force
  (J)   (N)   (m)

Kinetic energy is the energy an object has because of its movement. An object has more kinetic energy:

- the greater its mass
- the greater its speed.

kinetic energy (J) = $\frac{1}{2}$ × mass (kg) × speed^2 (m/s)

If you stretch a spring or a piece of **elastic**, before you let it go it has elastic **potential energy** stored in it. When you let it go, this energy is transferred as **kinetic energy**.

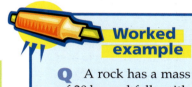

Worked example

Q A rock has a mass of 30 kg and falls with a speed of 20 m/s. What is its kinetic energy?

A kinetic energy
= $\frac{1}{2}$ mass × speed^2
= (0.5 × 30) × 20^2
= 15 × 400
= 6000 J

Questions

1 Find out your mass in kg. Multiply this figure by 10 to work out your weight in newtons.
2 A boat is floating on the water. Describe the forces that are acting on the boat.
3 A car reverses out of a parking space. Describe the forces acting on it.
4 An aeroplane is sent to deliver relief supplies to people without food. It is unable to land because of the dangers involved. It drops a 100 kg package that falls at 30 m/s. What is the kinetic energy of the package?

Friction and falling

Friction

The force of friction is always opposite to the direction in which an object is travelling. It slows the object down. When work is done against a frictional force, energy is transferred mainly as heat. Friction heats the object up and wears it away (for example, an aeroplane is both slowed down and heated up due to the friction of the air). The surface of an object may 'wear away' due to friction (for example, tyres on a car).

A force of friction acts:
- when an object moves through air or water
- when solid surfaces slide over one another.

Brakes use friction between solid surfaces to slow cars down. The greater the speed of a car:

- the greater the braking force needed to slow the car down in the same time; *or*
- the longer it takes to slow the car down, if you use the same braking force.

If you brake too hard then the car will skid as there is not enough friction between the car and the road surface.

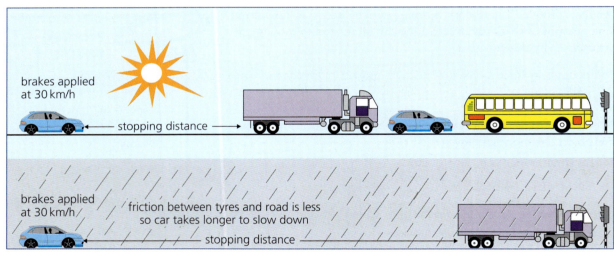

brakes applied at 30 km/h

← stopping distance →

brakes applied at 30 km/h

friction between tyres and road is less so car takes longer to slow down

← stopping distance →

Wet surfaces reduce friction

The stopping distance of a car depends on:
- the distance the car travels during the driver's 'thinking time'
- the distance travelled while the brakes are applied.

The stopping distance of a car increases if:
- the car is travelling faster
- the driver's reactions are slow (due to drink, drugs, tiredness)
- the road conditions are poor (wet, icy, poor visibility)
- the car is poorly maintained (worn brakes).

When a car has reached a steady speed, the frictional forces balance the driving force.

The faster something falls through air or a liquid, the greater the force of friction. When a body falls:

■ at first it accelerates due to the force of gravity

■ the force of friction eventually balances the force of gravity

■ the object now falls at **terminal velocity**, which is a steady speed.

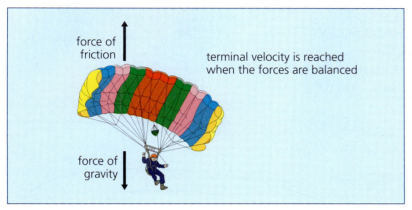

force of friction

terminal velocity is reached when the forces are balanced

force of gravity

Terminal velocity

1 N (newton) is the force needed to give a mass of 1 kg an acceleration of 1 m/s^2.

Force, mass and acceleration can all be linked in the following formula:

force (N) = **mass** (kg) × **acceleration** (m/s^2)

Worked example

Q A parachutist has a mass of 70 kg and accelerates at 8 m/s^2. What force is being exerted?

A force = mass × acceleration

$= 70 \times 8$

$= 560$ N

You may have to rearrange any equation in an examination.

Questions

1 A car slows down at a rate of 6 m/s^2. It has a weight of 10 000 N. What force is being applied to slow the car down?

2 Suggest **three** factors, in terms of road conditions, which increase the braking distance of a car.

3 A mountaineer dislodges a stone. At first the stone accelerates down the cliff-face. After a few seconds the stone falls at a steady speed. Explain what has happened.

Moving in space

Smaller bodies move around larger bodies in space. Planets and comets orbit the Sun, the Moon and satellites orbit the Earth. Like all bodies, they are attracted to each other by the force of **gravity**. As the distance between them gets larger, the force of gravity becomes disproportionately less. In other words, if the distance doubles then the force of gravity more than halves.

A smaller body stays in **orbit** around a larger one because of a combination of the gravity between the bodies and the speed of the object. The further away an orbiting body is from the larger body, the longer it takes to make one orbit.

The orbits of the planets are like squashed circles (**ellipses**) with the Sun quite close to the centre.

The planets we can see from Earth move slowly across the backdrop of stars. Their position depends on exactly where they, and the Earth, are in their orbits around the Sun.

> The Earth spins on its own axis once every 24 hours.
>
> The half of the Earth facing the Sun is in daylight; the other half is in night.
>
> The Earth orbits the Sun once every 365 days.

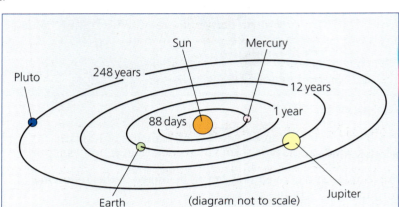

Planets orbit the Sun

Comets have orbits that are far from circular – sometimes they are much closer to the Sun than at other times. This is when we see them.

> Planets do not give out their own light. We see them because they reflect light from the Sun.

Satellites

For satellites to stay in orbit they must maintain a particular speed.

> Satellites are put into orbit around the Earth to:
> - send information between places a long way apart on the Earth
> - monitor conditions on Earth such as weather
> - observe the Universe without Earth's atmosphere getting in the way.

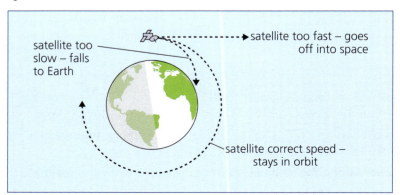

Staying in orbit

Communication satellites (for example, for television) are in orbit high above the equator. They move at the same speed as the Earth so that they always in the same place above the Earth. This is called a **geostationary orbit**. No more that 400 of these satellites can be put into orbit, otherwise they would interfere with the each other's signals.

Monitoring satellites scan the Earth to see what is going on. They are in a much lower **polar orbit**. They stay in one place as the Earth spins below. They scan the Earth once a day.

The origin of the Universe

Our Sun is one of many millions of stars in a group called the **Milky Way**. These stars are often many millions of times further away from us than the planets in our **solar system**.

The Universe is made up of at least a billion galaxies. **Galaxies** are often many millions of times further apart than stars within the galaxy.

The life history of a star • • • • • • • • • • • •

Stars, including the Sun, form when enough dust and gas from space is pulled together by gravitational attraction. Smaller masses also form and can be attracted by larger masses to become planets in orbit.

As stars are so massive:

- the force of gravity tends to draw the matter together
- the very high temperatures tend to make the star expand.

During the **stable** period (which may last for billions of years) these forces are balanced. Our Sun is at this stage in its life. However, the forces of expansion then begin to 'win' and the star expands and becomes a **red giant**. It now becomes so big that the forces of expansion decrease and the force of gravity becomes the stronger force.

The star now contracts under its own gravity to become a **white dwarf** and its matter may be millions of times denser than that of Earth. If the red giant is massive enough it may rapidly contract and then explode to become a **supernova**. Dust and gas are thrown into space and a very dense **neutron star** remains.

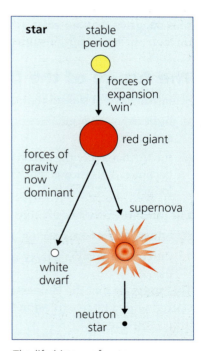

The life history of a star

Questions

1. Describe the pattern that links the distance a planet is from the Sun and how long it takes for one orbit.

2. How are satellites kept in geostationary orbit?

3. Why are monitoring satellites placed in a lower polar orbit?

4. Describe the life history of a star.

More about the Universe

Black holes

The material that forms a neutron star at the end of a star's life cycle may be so dense that nothing can escape from it. This includes light and other forms of electromagnetic radiation. This is a **black hole**. These cannot be seen but we can observe their effects. One effect is that gases from nearby stars may spiral into the black hole. The X-rays emitted can be detected.

The chemistry of stars

During a star's life the nuclei of lighter elements (mainly hydrogen and helium) gradually fuse together (nuclear fusion) to produce the nuclei of heavier elements. These reactions release a lot of energy, which is radiated by the stars.

Nuclei of the heaviest elements are present in the Sun and atoms of these elements are present in the inner planets of our solar system. This suggests that our solar system was formed from the material thrown out when earlier stars exploded.

The future of the Universe?

Scientists have observed that:

- light from other galaxies is shifted to the red end of the spectrum
- the further away the galaxy is, the greater this **'red shift'** becomes. This means that the wavelength of the light is becoming longer.

The current way of explaining this is that:

- other galaxies are moving away from us very quickly
- the further away a galaxy is, the faster it is moving away from us.

This suggests that the Universe is expanding and that it may have started with a huge explosion from one place. This is known as the **'big bang'** theory.

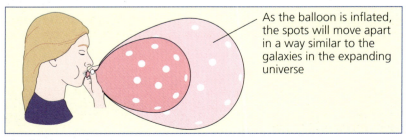

As the balloon is inflated, the spots will move apart in a way similar to the galaxies in the expanding universe

The 'big bang' theory

If the forces of expansion 'win' then the Universe will continue to expand. If gravity eventually overcomes the forces of expansion, then the Universe will crunch together again.

Is there life out there?

People have always wanted to know if there is life on other planets in our solar system or around other stars. There are three ways of trying to find out.

■ We may be able to see living organisms such as microorganisims by going, for example, to Mars or Europa (a moon of Jupiter). Robots can be used to send pictures or collect samples. These collections may show fossilised remains.

■ Living organisms cause changes in the atmosphere. On Earth, for example, plants produce a large amount of oxygen. If we could detect similar changes in other atmospheres, and show that they were nothing to do with geology or other chemical reactions, then this would suggest that living organisms have been present.

■ We might be able to detect signals or communicate with other life forms that have technologies as advanced as our own. The search for extra-terrestrial intelligence (SETI) has used radio telescopes to try to detect meaningful signals (not just 'noise') for more than 40 years.

None of these methods has yet given us any proof of life in other places, but the search continues.

A study of a Martian meteorite has found evidence that primitive life may once have existed on Mars. Scientists have discovered tiny crystals of magnetite. These crystals are identical to those made by a type of bacteria on Earth. They are quite different to the mineral magnetite found in rocks. These scientists argue that it is not possible to produce these crystals in any way other than by bacteria, so there must once have been bacteria on Mars. Other scientists are not so sure!

Other studies of Mars suggest that there once might have been water. Although the climate is now freezing, it was thought that Mars was once warm because of volcanic activity. Its atmosphere is mainly carbon dioxide. So it was very similar to Earth before plants evolved (see pages 58–59). We know that primitive microorganisms existed on Earth then, so is it possible that they might have been present on Mars too?

Questions

1 What evidence is there that the Universe is getting bigger?

2 What is meant by the 'red shift'?

3 What is a black hole?

4 Why might changes in the atmosphere of a planet indicate the presence of life?

Terminal exam questions

1 This question is about machines in a fitness centre.

a The diagrams show a student using a rowing machine and its display panel. The display panel shows the readings at the end of the exercise.

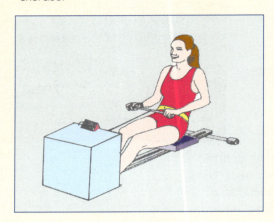

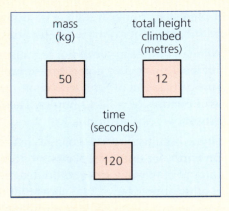

mass (kg)	total height climbed (metres)
50	12

time (seconds)
120

The equation below is used to calculate weight

weight = mass × gravitational field strength
(newton, N)   (kilogram, kg)   (newton/kilogram, N/kg)

Use this equation to help you calculate the work done by the student during the exercise   [4]

6 marks

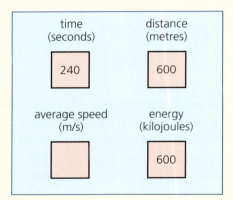

time (seconds)	distance (metres)
240	600

average speed (m/s)	energy (kilojoules)
	600

Calculate the missing reading on the display panel.   [2]

b The diagrams show a student using a step machine and its display panel. The display panel shows the readings at the end of the exercise.

2 The diagram shows a satellite in orbit around the Earth.

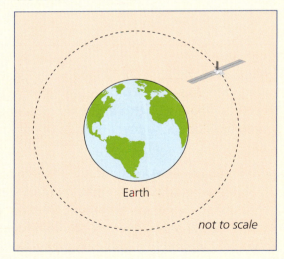

Earth

not to scale

a i Explain why the satellite stays in orbit   [2]
  ii The satellite is boosted to a higher orbit. What effect will this have on the time the satellite takes to complete one orbit?   [1]

b Communication satellites send information between places that are a long way apart on Earth.
  i In what type of orbit are communication satellites usually placed?   [1]
  ii Explain why they are placed in this type of orbit.   [1]

c Monitoring satellites are used to monitor conditions on Earth, including the weather.
  i In what type of orbit are weather satellites usually placed? [1]
  ii Explain why they are placed in this kind of orbit [1]

7 marks

3 A cliff railway links the villages of Lynton and Lynmouth in Devon. The railway has two cars that run on parallel tracks. The cars are joined by a continuous cable that runs around two large pulley wheels. One pulley wheel is at the top and the other at the bottom of the cliff. Each car has a tank which holds water. As water is run out of the tank in the lower car, the upper car descends pulling the lower car up the cliff. The diagram shows the lower car stationary.

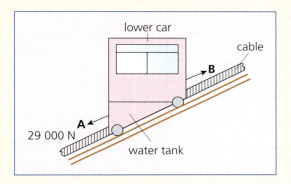

a The brakes of both cars are released. At first the cars do not move. Write down the magnitude (size) of force **B** [1]

b Water is run out of the tank in the lower car.
  i What then happens to the magnitude (size) of force **A**? [1]
  ii The car then starts to move. Explain why. [1]

c After a while the car moves up the cliff at a steady speed. How does force **A** compare to force **B** as the car moves up the cliff at a steady speed? [1]

d Forces are measured in newtons. Complete the sentence below to give the definition of one newton.
  One newton is the force needed to give a .... . [2]

6 marks
Total for test: 19 marks

Waves and their properties

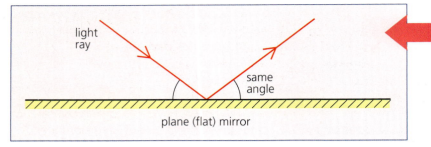

Reflection

You have already learned how light and sound behave like waves. Here is a reminder – you need to remember this, but will not be tested on it in an examination.

When sound waves are reflected from a hard surface, they are bounced back as echoes.

When a ray of light is reflected from a flat, shiny surface (for example, a plane mirror), the angle it leaves the surface is the same as the angle at which it hits the surface.

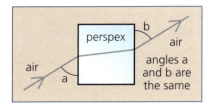
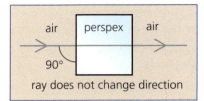

Refraction

If a ray of light crosses from one transparent substance into another (for example, from air into glass) then the ray usually changes direction – it refracts.

The only time it does not change direction is when it meets the boundary between the two substances at right angles, along a normal (that is, a line perpendicular to the boundary).

Other types of wave

There are other sorts of waves. You can produce them in ropes and springs as well as ripples on the surface of a pond.

Waves travelling along a rope, along a spring or across water can be reflected. Waves travelling across water can also be refracted if the wave enters a deeper or a shallower area (unless their direction of travel is along the normal).

It is the change in speed of the waves of water (as they cross the boundary from deeper to shallower water) that causes the change in direction.

This behaviour shown by waves suggests that:

- light and sound also travel as waves
- light and sound waves are refracted, because they will travel at different speeds as they cross a boundary from one substance to another.

Sound is also refracted in this way. Sound waves change direction when they cross the boundary between different substances at angles less than a right angle.

How waves travel

A wave is a regular pattern of disturbances, usually through a substance such as water, air, rope, a spring and so on. Only light waves are able to travel through a vacuum (that is, they do not need to be carried by any substance).

A wave moves energy from one place to another without transferring any matter. So, for example, a wave travelling through a spring does not carry the metal from the beginning to the end of the spring.

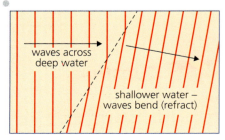

Waves refract

Types of wave movement

There are two types of wave movement.

Transverse waves

The disturbances in transverse waves travel at right angles to the direction that the wave is travelling. This is what you probably imagine when you think of a wave. Waves through water and rope travel this way. Light waves are also transverse waves. They can travel through the vacuum as they do not require a medium.

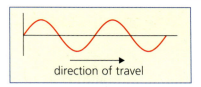

A transverse wave

Longitudinal waves

The disturbances are in the direction of travel. This is the way that waves travel through springs. It is also the way that sound waves travel through solids, liquids and gases.

A longitudinal wave

Measuring waves

You need to know three things about waves: their height, length and frequency. These can most easily be seen on a transverse wave.

- The height (maximum disturbance) of the wave is called its **amplitude**.

- The distance between a particular point on one 'peak' of the wave and the next is the **wavelength**.

- The number of waves passing a particular point each second (or produced by the source) is the **frequency**. This is measured in **hertz** (Hz).

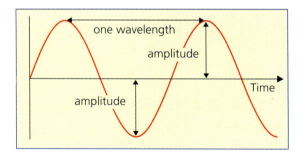

All of these measures also apply to longitudinal waves.

Wave speed

The speed at which a wave is travelling can be found by:

wave speed (m/s) = frequency (Hz) × wavelength (m)

Worked example

Q A wave has a speed of 50 m/s and a frequency of 10 hertz. What is the wavelength of the wave?

A $\text{wavelength} = \dfrac{\text{wave speed}}{\text{frequency}} = \dfrac{50}{10} = 5\,\text{m}$

Questions

1 When you stand in water up to your knees, the lower half of your legs look shorter and 'bent'. Explain this.

2 Draw a transverse wave. Mark on your diagram the amplitude and wavelength of your wave.

More properties of waves

Diffraction

When a wave moves through a gap or spreads out as it passes an obstacle, the wave spreads out from the edges. This is called **diffraction**.

Electromagnetic radiation and sound can be diffracted. This supports the idea that they travel as waves.

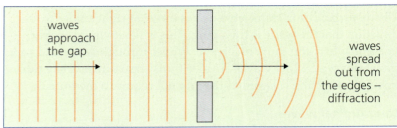

It is because of diffraction that:

■ sounds may be heard in the shadow of buildings (around corners)

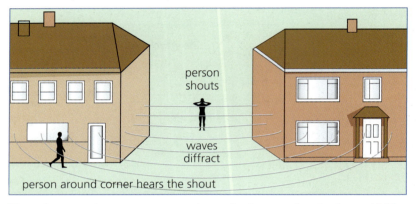

■ radio signals can sometimes be picked up in the shadow of hills.

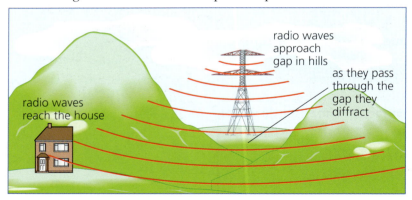

Internal reflection

When a ray of light travels from glass, perspex or water into the air, some of the light is also reflected from the boundary. This is called **internal reflection**.

If the angle between the light ray and the normal is greater than a certain **critical angle** (different for different substances), then **total internal reflection** occurs.

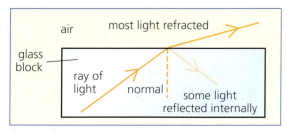

Internal reflection

Uses of waves

Optical fibres

Optical fibres work by using total internal reflection. For example, endoscopes containing optical fibres are used by doctors to see into parts of patients' bodies such as the gut and blood vessels. Light stays in the optical fibre until it comes out of the other end.

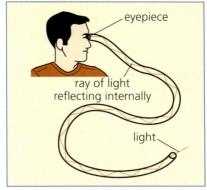

Using an endoscope

Analogue and digital signals

Speech and music can be converted into electrical signals and carried long distances through cables, or by using electromagnetic waves as carriers. This is how most televisions and radios work. Information can also be converted into light or infra red signals and sent (by total internal reflection) along optical fibres. This is how cable television works.

Analogue signals vary in amplitude and frequency, just like speech and music. As the signals travel they weaken and other random signals ('noise') can be picked up. Different frequencies weaken to different extents. Each time an analogue signal is amplified, these differences and any noise picked up along the way are also amplified. This means that the quality of the signal gets less and less like the original. The picture on the TV screen or the sound from your radio becomes 'fuzzy'.

Digital signals are coded as a series of pulses. There is no variation in amplitude or frequency. The signal is either 'on' or 'off'. Digital signals have two main advantages over analogue signals:

- They have a higher quality – there is no change in them as they are transmitted. Even though the pulses themselves may weaken, they are still recognised as 'on' or 'off', so the quality of the signal is maintained during transmission.

- More information can be sent at the same time – whether it is through cable, optical fibre or carrier wave.

This is why you have to 'tune' your radio to receive particular frequencies of radio waves (for example, BBC Radio 1 is 97.6–99.8 FM).

Digital television is gradually replacing analogue. It can offer many more programmes at the same time, and with a much better quality picture.

Questions

1. A doctor is able to use an endoscope to see into your gut. Explain, in your own words, how this is possible.

2. You are watching the waves come through a narrow harbour entrance. You notice that the small boats inside the harbour wall are 'bobbing' up and down. Explain why they are doing this.

3. Why do digital signals result in a clearer picture on a television screen?

Using reflection and refraction

Ultrasound

A vibrating object produces a sound. The greater the amplitude (size) of the vibrations, the louder the sound.

The number of complete vibrations per second is the frequency (hertz). The higher the frequency, the higher the **pitch** of the sound.

The pitch of a sound is a measure of how high or low it sounds

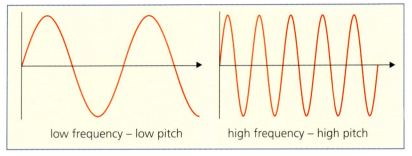

low frequency – low pitch   high frequency – high pitch

An electronic system can be used to produce electrical oscillations with any frequency, and these can be used to produce **ultrasonic waves**. Their frequency is higher than humans can hear.

Ultrasound is used:

- in industry – for cleaning and quality control (for example, detecting flaws in metals, perhaps in bridges)
- in medicine – for pre-natal scanning (forming pictures of the baby in the womb)
- in liquids – for cleaning delicate instruments without having to take them apart.

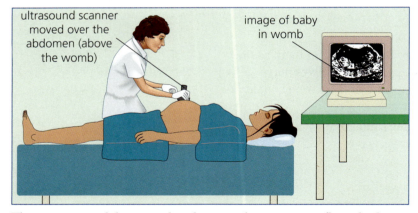

ultrasound scanner moved over the abdomen (above the womb)

image of baby in womb

These scans work because the ultrasound waves are reflected when they meet a boundary between two different media (for example, the growing baby and the fluid in the womb). The time taken for the reflections of ultrasonic pulses to reach a detector is a measure of how far away this boundary is. The detector is placed near to the source. Information about the time taken for reflections to travel is usually presented as a visual display of the body or the object being scanned.

Earthquakes

An earthquake produces shock waves. These are seismic waves and have been used to study the structure of the Earth. Seismographs detect the waves.

There are two types of wave:

- P waves are fast, longitudinal and travel through liquids and solids
- S waves are slower, transverse and travel only through liquids.

Both types travel faster through denser materials.

- If the density of the material changes gradually then the waves travel in a curved path.
- If the density changes quickly then the direction of the waves changes abruptly.

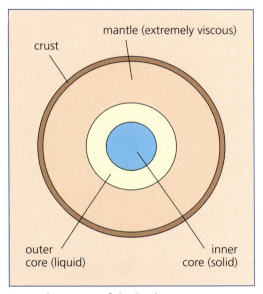

Layered structure of the Earth

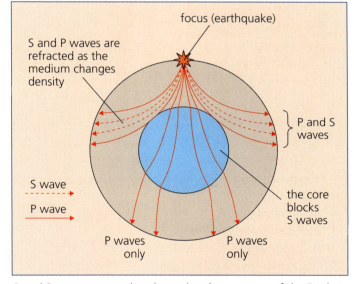

P and S waves are used to determine the structure of the Earth

If the paths of these waves are observed, then the results suggest the Earth has a layered structure with:

- a thin crust
- an extremely viscous mantle (density increasing with depth) that goes almost half way to the centre of the Earth
- a core, just over half of the Earth's diameter – outer part liquid, inner part solid.

Questions

1   When engineers use ultrasonic waves to check bridges, what do you think they are checking?

2   How are both P and S waves used to determine the structure of the Earth?
Explain your answer in terms of the nature of the waves and in terms of refraction.

Electromagnetic radiation

The colours of white light are refracted at different angles because they have different wavelengths.

red — least refracted
orange
yellow
green
blue
indigo
violet — most refracted

white light

If you pass white light through a prism, the light splits into different colours because each colour is refracted to a different extent. This results in a spectrum of light that has the same colours (and in the same order) as a rainbow.

Light is only one type of **electromagnetic radiation**. There are other types that you cannot see. They form a continuous spectrum. All types of electromagnetic radiation travel at the same speed (the 'speed of light') through space (a vacuum).

highest frequency   shortest wavelength

gamma rays
X-rays
ultraviolet rays
light
infra red rays
microwaves
radio waves

lowest frequency   longest wavelength

Different wavelengths are reflected, absorbed or transmitted in different ways, depending on the substance and the type of surface. When electromagnetic radiation is absorbed by an object or a surface:

- it makes the substance hotter
- it may create an alternating electric current with the same frequency as the radiation itself.

The uses and the effects of the different types of radiation depend on these properties as well as others.

The dangers of each type of electromagnetic radiation are dealt with on page 124.

Uses of electromagnetic radiation • • • •

Radio waves

Radio waves are used to transmit radio and television programmes across the Earth. The longer wavelength radio waves are reflected back down to Earth by an electrically charged layer in the upper atmosphere. It is therefore possible to send these waves long distances, despite the curvature of the Earth.

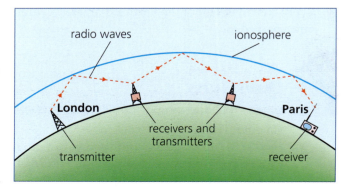

radio waves   ionosphere

London   **Paris**

receivers and transmitters

transmitter   receiver

Microwave radiation

Microwave radiation has wavelengths that can easily pass through the Earth's atmosphere. It is therefore used to send information to and from satellites in orbit and within phone networks. This type of radiation has wavelengths strongly absorbed by water molecules, so is used in microwave cooking.

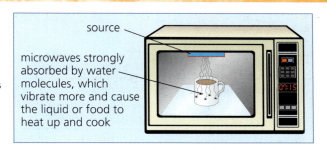

source

microwaves strongly absorbed by water molecules, which vibrate more and cause the liquid or food to heat up and cook

Infra red radiation

Infra red radiation is used in grills, toasters and radiant heaters (for example, electric fires). It is also used in optical fibre communications and for television and video remote controls.

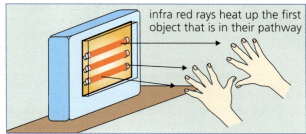

infra red rays heat up the first object that is in their pathway

Ultraviolet radiation

Some people use ultraviolet radiation to get a sun tan on a sun bed. We can get a natural tan from the Sun's UV radiation. Special coatings, which absorb UV radiation and then emit it as light, are used in fluorescent lamps and in security coding.

UV light

X-radiation

X-radiation is used in X-rays. These can be 'shadow' pictures of bones or metals. These pictures can be used to identify broken bones or problems in metal structures.

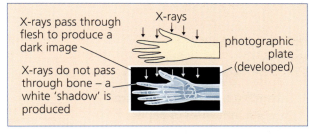

X-rays

X-rays pass through flesh to produce a dark image

photographic plate (developed)

X-rays do not pass through bone – a white 'shadow' is produced

Gamma radiation

Gamma radiation has several uses:

- ■ to kill harmful bacteria in food and make it sterile
- ■ to sterilise surgical instruments
- ■ to kill cancer cells.

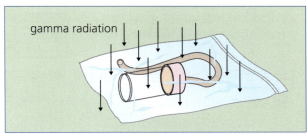

gamma radiation

Questions

1 List the following types of electromagnetic radiation from that with the shortest wavelength to that with the longest: UV, X-rays, microwaves and radio waves.

2 Give **two** uses of infra red radiation.

3 Explain how, in the UK, we were able to listen to commentary of the Olympic Games in Sydney on long-wave radios.

Dangers of radiation

Type of radiation	Dangers of exposure	How to reduce exposure
Microwaves	Absorbed by water in living cells. Causes the cells to heat up and be killed or damaged	Make sure that the seals around the door are good.
Infra red radiation	Absorbed by the skin and felt as heat	Do not stay in the Sun too long
Ultraviolet radiation	Passes through the skin to deeper tissues. High doses can cause cells to become cancerous	Darker skins have natural UV protection. Wearing UV filter sun lotions can help reduce the risks of sunburn and damage to skin
X-rays	Mostly go straight through the skin and soft tissues, but some absorbed by cells. High doses can kill cells. Low doses can cause cells to become cancerous	If taking X-rays, stay well away from the source. As a patient, you should not be X-rayed too often
Gamma rays	Mostly go straight through the skin and soft tissues, but some absorbed by cells. High doses can kill cells. Low doses can cause cells to become cancerous	Enclose the source in a thick, lead-lined container

Radioactive substances

Some substances give out radiation all of the time. There are three types of radiation emitted by these radioactive substances:

- **alpha radiation** – easily absorbed by a few centimetres of air or a thin sheet of paper
- **beta radiation** – passes through paper but will be absorbed by a few millimetres of metal
- **gamma radiation** – very penetrating and requires many centimetres of lead or several metres of concrete to stop it.

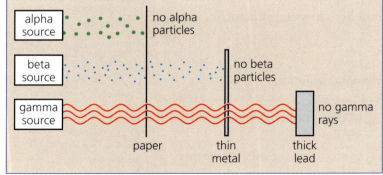

How do we explain this? The three types of radiation are all different:

- alpha (α) particles are the same as a helium nucleus – they consist of 2 protons and 2 neutrons
- beta (β) particles are very fast-moving electrons – for each beta particle emitted by a radioactive substance, one proton becomes one neutron
- gamma (γ) rays are very short wavelength electromagnetic radiation – no particles are emitted.

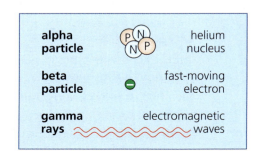

When a radioactive substance emits alpha or beta particles, its atoms change from one element to another (because the number of protons changes). For example:

- radium $^{226}_{88}$Ra loses an alpha particle ($^4_2$He) and becomes radon $^{222}_{86}$Rn

- polonium $^{218}_{84}$Po loses a beta particle ($^0_{-1}$e) and becomes astatine $^{218}_{85}$At.

There are radioactive substances all around us. They are in the ground, the air, building materials and food. We also receive radiation from space. All of this we call **background radiation**.

When radiation collides with neutral atoms or molecules then these may become **ionised** (charged). If this happens in living cells cancers may result. Alpha particles are strongly ionising. The larger the dose of radiation, the greater the risk. Even higher doses of radiation can be used to kill cancer cells or harmful microorganisms.

The **dangers of radiation** to humans depend on whether the source is outside or inside the body (see table).

Workers at risk from radiation wear a special badge to check the amount of radiation they have been exposed to. The greater the exposure, the darker the photographic film in the badge becomes.

Source outside the body	Source inside the body
beta and gamma radiation are the most dangerous as they can pass into the body and be absorbed by cells and therefore damage them	alpha radiation becomes the most dangerous as it is strongly absorbed by cells and is strongly ionising
alpha radiation is unlikely to reach the cells	beta and gamma radiation are less dangerous as they are less strongly absorbed

Using radiation

Certain substances will absorb different forms of radiation. This means that a radioactive source can be used to monitor or control the thickness of materials manufactured in industry (for example, paper).

- If the paper is too thick, not enough alpha particles will pass through to the detector so the rollers are adjusted to make the paper thinner.

- If the paper is too thin, too many alpha particles are detected so the rollers are adjusted to make the paper thicker.

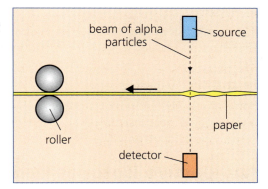

Questions

1 Studies have suggested that microwaves from mobile phones may affect the brains of regular users. What damage could high doses of microwaves do to brain cells?

2 Alpha radiation is used to check the thickness of paper. Why are gamma or beta radiation sources not used?

3 The following sequence shows the radioactive decay of plutonium 242 to uranium 234:
$^{242}_{94}$Pu → $^{238}_{92}$U → $^{234}_{90}$Th → $^{234}_{91}$Pa → $^{234}_{92}$U
How does uranium decay to thorium (Th)?
How does thorium decay to protactinium (Pa)?

Radioactive decay

Decay is a result of changes in the nucleus of an atom. Before you can understand radioactive decay, you need first to understand the structure of the atoms from which radioactive substances are made.

Theories of the atom

One early theory was the 'plum pudding model'. This described the atom as a positively charged sphere with negative electrons studded throughout, like raisins in a pudding. In 1911 Rutherford and Marsden carried out an experiment in which they fired alpha particles at a very thin piece of gold foil. Most of the alpha particles went straight through, but a few were scattered at wide angles by the foil. They worked out that this could only be explained if all the positive charge was concentrated in the nucleus of the atom, not throughout the atom as in the plum pudding model. They calculated the size of the nucleus from the scatter patterns and found that it was a minute part of the atom. If an atom was the size of a school hall, its nucleus would be the size of a full stop! This work led to our current view of the atom.

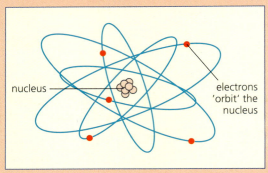

The structure of an atom

Atoms are made up of protons and neutrons in the nucleus with electrons orbiting the nucleus.

An atom has no charge. It has the same number of protons as electrons.

The number of protons in an atom determines what element it is (For example, carbon always has 6, sodium always has 11).

The mass number of an element equals the number of protons and neutrons in the nucleus.

Some atoms have different numbers of neutrons. Chlorine has always got 17 protons. However, some forms have 18 neutrons and some have 20 neutrons. These are **isotopes** of chlorine.

Radioactive isotopes (radionuclides)

These have atoms with unstable nuclei. When an unstable nucleus breaks down (disintegrates):

- it emits radiation
- a different atom, with a different number of protons, results.

The older the material, the less radiation it emits. It will have passed through several half-lives.

Half-life

The **half-life** of a radioactive source is the time taken for the number of radioactive atoms to half. In other words, for the substance to become half as radioactive.

For example, the half-life of substance X = 100 years:

■ after 50 years it is half as radioactive

■ after another 50 years it has lost another half of its radioactivity and is only 25% as radioactive as when it was formed.

The graph shows this.

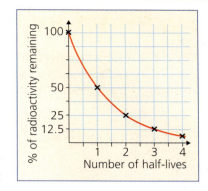

Uranium atoms have a very long half-life. They decay through a series of isotopes with short half-lives. Eventually they produce stable isotopes of lead.

If you want to date an igneous rock you can do this by working out the relative proportions of uranium and lead in the rock.

You can also use a radioisotope of potassium (potassium 40) to date rocks. It breaks down to argon. If the argon remains trapped in the igneous rock, then again you can work out the proportions and date the rock.

The nuclear process

This involves splitting atoms – a process known as **nuclear fission**. An atom with a very large nucleus is bombarded with neutrons. This results in:

■ the nucleus splitting into two smaller nuclei

■ further neutrons being released – these may cause further nuclear fission and could lead to a 'chain' reaction (rods can be placed between the nuclear material to stop the chain reaction 'getting out of hand')

■ new atoms being formed that are also radioactive.

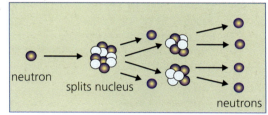

A nuclear chain reaction

The energy released during nuclear fission is very large compared to that released when a chemical bond is made between two atoms.

Worked example

Q When a tree is alive, as well as taking in carbon 12 it takes in a proportion of radioactive carbon 14. The half-life of carbon 14 is 5700 years. Once the tree dies, it stops taking in carbon 14 and the radioactive carbon already in the tree decays.

A tree is found where only 25% of the original carbon 14 is still present. How old is the tree?

A After one half-life, 50% of the carbon 14 is present. Therefore, after two half-lives only 25% will be present.
Two half-lives is 2 × 5700 years.
The tree is approximately 11 400 years old.

Questions

1 A substance has a half-life of 100 years. How long will it be before three quarters of its radioactivity has been lost?

2 How many protons, neutrons and electrons does $^{238}_{92}U$ have?

3 A radioactive source has a half-life of 70 years. How much of the original radioactivity will remain after 140 years?

Terminal exam questions

1 Wave ripples are crossing a pond as shown in the diagram.

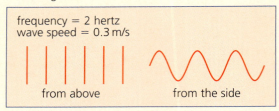

frequency = 2 hertz
wave speed = 0.3 m/s

from above   from the side

a Are the waves transverse or longitudinal?
Explain your answer. [3]
b i What is the wavelength of the waves? [4]
ii Copy this diagram. Mark one wavelength.
[1]

c The waves pass through a gap between two wooden blocks as shown in this diagram.

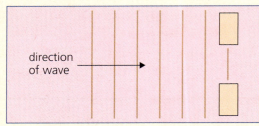

direction of wave

i Copy and complete the diagram to show what would happen to the waves. [1]
ii Why would the direction of the waves change if the water suddenly became deeper? [2]

11 marks

2 a Radioactive substances can emit three different types of radiation. The following diagrams represent two investigations of radioactive sources.

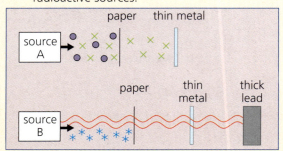

paper   thin metal

source A

paper   thin metal   thick lead

source B

i What type(s) of radiation is source A emitting? [2]
ii What type(s) of radiation is source B emitting? [2]
b i Under what conditions is alpha radiation the most dangerous to the body? Explain your answer. [3]
ii What are alpha particles? [3]
c Suggest **two** uses of radiation in a hospital. [2]
d The following table illustrates the radioactivity of a source.

Seconds	Particles emitted per minute
0	1000
50	750
100	500
150	375
200	250

i What is the half-life of the substance? [1]
ii After what period of time will the emissions have reduced to 125 per minute? [1]
iii How many half-lives does this represent? [1]

15 marks

3 Earthquakes produce shock waves.
a How are these shock waves detected? [1]
Use this diagram and labels X, Y and Z to help answer the questions which follow.

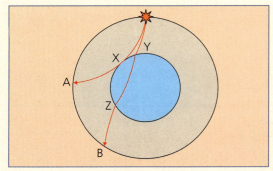

b i Describe and explain the path of wave A. [4]
ii Describe and explain the path of wave B. [2]
iii What type of wave are waves A and B? [2]

9 marks

4 a A ray of light passes into a perspex block from the air.

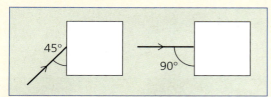

Copy and complete the diagrams to show the path of the rays as they pass through the blocks and back into the air. [3]

b You can use a prism to split up the colours in white light.
   Why do the colours separate as they pass through the prism? [2]

c i What is an endoscope used for? [2]
  ii How does the endoscope work? [4]

d Light is part of the electromagnetic spectrum.
  i What is meant by electromagnetic radiation? [2]
  ii Copy and complete the following diagrams by placing the types of electromagnetic radiation listed in sequence 1–4 against the arrows.

gamma rays   **microwaves**
light rays   **UV rays**

Highest frequency   ↑ 1
                   2
                   3
Lowest frequency   4   [3]

light rays   **X-rays**
radio waves   **infra red waves**

Shortest wavelength ↑ 1
                    2
                    3
Longest wavelength   4   [3]

19 marks

5 Study the graph which shows the radioactive decay of a substance.

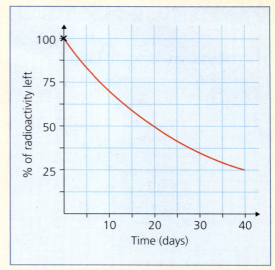

a i How much radioactivity is left after 30 days? [1]
  ii After how many days will $\frac{1}{32}$ of its initial radioactivity be left? [1]

b How are radioisotopes used to date rocks? [3]

c Gamma radiation has a number of uses. State **three** of them. [3]

d Microwaves are a different form of electromagnetic radiation.
   How do microwaves heat up food? [3]

11 marks
Total for test: 65 marks

Answers to module test and terminal exam questions

Humans as organisms

Question	Answer	Marks	Total
1	1 red cells 2 plasma 3 platelets 4 white cells	1 1 1 1	4
2	1 flattens 2 contracts 3 increases 4 decreases	1 1 1 1	4
3	1 stomach 2 liver 3 large intestine 4 pancreas	1 1 1 1	4
4	B and C	2	2
5	A and D	2	2

Question		Answer	Marks	Total
6	1.	A	1	
	2.	D	1	
	3.	C	1	
	4.	C	1	4
7	1.	B	1	
	2.	C	1	
	3.	C	1	
	4.	C	1	4
8	1.	D	1	
	2.	B	1	
	3.	A	1	
	4.	D	1	4

Total for test: 28 marks

Maintenance of life

Question	Answer	Marks	Total
1	1 chloroplast 2 nucleus 3 cell wall 4 cytoplasm	1 1 1 1	4
2	1 carbon dioxide 2 nitrates 3 sugars 4 potassium	1 1 1 1	4
3	1 effector 2 receptor 3 sensory neurone 4 relay neurone	1 1 1 1	4
4	D and E	2	2
5	B and E *many pupils confuse glycogen and glucagon*	2	2

Question		Answer	Marks	Total
6	1.	A	1	
	2.	C	1	
	3.	A	1	
	4.	B	1	4
7	1.	A	1	
	2.	C	1	
	3.	D	1	
	4.	A	1	4
8	1.	C	1	
	2.	A	1	
	3.	A	1	
	4.	D	1	4

Total for test: 28 marks

Environment

Question			Answer	Marks	Total
1	a	i	Vole/small bird/beetle.	1	
		ii	There are small numbers of trees compared to the animals	1	
			but the trees' mass is very much greater	1	
			one tree can support many animals.	1	
	b		*Any eight points from*: • made into sugars/carbohydrates • made into fats • made into proteins • makes plant structures • eaten by animal • made into animal structures • lost from animal or plant through respiration • as carbon dioxide • animal may die • decomposed • by microorganisms • microorganisms respire • release carbon dioxide. *These are the general ideas – you do not have to use the exact words.*	8	
	c		*Any five points from*: • plant dies • decomposed • by microorganisms/bacteria/fungi • nitrogen in plant converted to ammonia/ammonium compounds • ammonium compounds converted to nitrates • by nitrifying bacteria • taken up by another plant. *The ideas would have to be in a logical sequence to obtain full marks.*	5	
	d		Some energy is transferred to the production of waste	1	
			chemical energy in respiration	1	
			heat energy and	1	
			kinetic (movement) energy.	1	**21 marks**
2	a		*Any six points (in a reasonably logical sequence) from*: • plants continue to grow quickly • many die • due to competition/not enough light • decompose • microorganisms use up oxygen • to respire • fish die • through suffocation. *Alternative answers referring to the drying out of the pond would receive marks – although this is not on the syllabus, it is correct. For example:* • plants die • they sink to the bottom • the layer of dead plants builds up • eventually wetland/marsh-loving plants may grow • these take up water and further dry out the pond • meadowland plants and then trees may establish.	6	
					6 marks

Question			Answer	Marks	Total
3	a	i	Carbon dioxide and methane.	2	
		ii	*Any three correct points (max. of 2 marks for each gas) from:* • methane – more cattle • methane – more rice fields • carbon dioxide – more people • carbon dioxide – more industry • carbon dioxide – more cars/burning of fossil fuel.	3	
		iii	More carbon dioxide in the air absorbs more of the Sun's energy less is reflected back into space the Earth warms up.	1 1 1	
	b	i	*Any two from:* • sulphur dioxide • nitrogen oxide(s) • carbon dioxide.	2	
		ii	*Any four points from:* • may damage buildings • will damage trees/other plants • will get into lakes/ponds/rivers • makes the water acidic • kills animals/plants in the water.	4	**14 marks**
4	a		Vegetation → snail → partridge → humans *Note: there are several other examples but the example must come from this food web.*	1	
	b	i	Vegetation.	1	
		ii	It will increase as there is more food so more young can be reared.	1 1 1	
		iii	They might increase as there is more vegetation to eat or they might decrease as thrushes may eat them instead of snails.	1 1 1 1	
	c		Total amount of food available competition for food predation disease.	1 1 1 1	**13 marks**
5	a	i	Photosynthesis.	1	
		ii	*Any three from:* • oxygen • fats • proteins • carbohydrates *or* sugar *or* starch.	3	
	b	i	Respiration.	1	
		ii	Water.	1	
	c		Bacteria and fungi *(or microorganisms for 1 mark)* decay *or* break down rabbit during respiration.	1 1 1 1	
	d		Climate changes sea level rises.	1 1	**12 marks**

Total for test: 66 marks

Inheritance and selection

Question			Answer	Marks	Total
1	a		Mitosis results in two cells and meiosis four cells.	1	
			Mitosis cells genetically the same, meiosis they are different.	1	
	b		Chromosomes all the same as parent's	1	
			so genetically identical.	1	
	c	i	You choose the male and female	1	
			with the best characteristics	1	
			so the offspring inherit these characteristics.	1	
		ii	Reduction in the number of gene types in the population	1	
			if a change in circumstances/environment,	1	
			for example temperature drops, new disease	1	
			and species can't adapt.	1	**11 marks**
2	a	i	Artificially altering the genetic make-up of an organism.	1	
		ii	Cut the gene	1	
			from the chromosome	1	
			and place in other species.	1	
		iii	Place genes in bacteria	1	
			that produce the protein	1	
			insulin.	1	
	b		Two alleles/genes	1	
			controlling the same characteristic	1	
			are different.	1	
	c	i	The nervous system.	1	
		ii			

Hh   Hh   [1]

H   h   H   h

HH   Hh   hH   hh   [1]

at risk   [1]   75% chance [1]

				4	**15 marks**
3	a	i	Tissue culture	1	
			embryo transplant.	1	
		ii	Tissue culture:		
			small group of cells from an organism	1	
			grown into a new organism.	1	
			Embryo transplant – *any two from*:		
			• cells from a developing embryo		
			• transplanted into host organism		
			• before the cells have become specialised.	2	
	b				

Cc   CC   [1]

C   c   C   C

CC   CC   cC   cC   [1]

no children cc   [1]   0% chance [1]

Note: it is better to draw a genetic diagram

| | | | | 4 | **10 marks** |

Question			Answer	Marks	Total
4			Wide variation in a species	1	
			weakest do not survive	1	
			for example, caught and eaten/easily catch disease	1	
			best adapted left to breed	1	
			so the species evolves.	1	**5 marks**
5	a	i	A gene that masks the affect of another.	1	
		ii	Pairs of genes	1	
			controlling the same characteristic.	1	
	b	i	At **A** the chromosomes replicate (are copied).	1	
			At **B** four new cells are produced each with:		
			half the original number of chromosomes	1	
			one chromosome from each original pair.	1	
		ii	To produce sex cells.	1	
	c	i	Ss × SS [1] No chance of sickle cell anaemia	1	
			S s S S [1] 50% chance of being a carrier.	1	
			SS sS sS SS [1]	3	
		ii	Helps prevent malaria.	1	
	d		*Any four points from*:		
			• chromosomes contain DNA		
			• genes are short lengths of DNA		
			• DNA codes for amino acids		
			• proteins give us our characteristics.	4	**17 marks**
6	a	i	**A** FSH	1	
			stimulates egg production	1	
			B oestrogen	1	
			now stops FSH production	1	
			C LH	1	
			causes the release of the egg.	1	
		ii	Pituitary gland.	1	
	b	i	FSH.	1	
		ii	Oestrogen (*progesterone is also correct*).	1	**9 marks**

Total for test: 67 marks

Metals

Question	Answer	Marks	Total
1	1 aluminium 2 carbon 3 iron 4 gold	1 1 1 1	 4
2	1 NaCl 2 Na_2O 3 $NaNO_3$ 4 Na_2SO_4	1 1 1 1	 4
3	1 neutralisation 2 reduction 3 oxidation 4 displacement	1 1 1 1	 4
4	A and C	2	2
5	A and E	2	2

Question	Answer		Marks	Total
6	1.	C	1	
	2.	B	1	
	3.	A	1	
	4.	C	1	4
7	1.	C	1	
	2.	B	1	
	3.	B	1	
	4.	D	1	4
8	1.	A	1	
	2.	D	1	
	3.	C	1	
	4.	B	1	4

Total for test: 28 marks

Earth materials

Question	Answer	Marks	Total
1	1 sedimentary 2 metamorphic 3 magma 4 igneous	1 1 1 1	 4
2	1 carbon dioxide 2 ammonia 3 nitrogen 4 ozone	1 1 1 1	 4
3	A and E	2	2
4	C and E	2	2
5	1. A 2. B 3. D 4. B	1 1 1 1	 4

Question	Answer		Marks	Total
6	1.	B	1	
	2.	D	1	
	3.	B	1	
	4.	C	1	4
7	1.	C	1	
	2.	C	1	
	3.	D	1	
	4.	C	1	4

Total for test: 24 marks

Patterns of chemical change

Question			Answer	Marks	Total
1	a	i	$3H_2$	1	
			$2NH_3$	1	
		ii	200 atmospheres pressure	1	
			450 °C	1	
			Iron catalyst.	1	
		iii	Reaction is reversible	1	
			so ammonia formed could break down.	1	
			These conditions ensure maximum ammonia production.	1	
	b	i	$2 \times N = 28 +$		
			$4 \times H = 4 +$		
			$3 \times O = 48$ answer $= 80$	1	
		ii	M_r of ammonia is 17 and M_r of ammonium nitrate is 80	1	
			therefore 17 tonnes of ammonia will produce 80 tonnes of ammonium nitrate.	1	
			85 tonnes of ammonia is five times this amount	1	
			so 5×80 tonnes will be produced $= 400$ tonnes	1	**13 marks**
2	a	i	Bonds broken:		
			4 C—H bonds at 413 $= 1652 +$		
			1 C=C bond at 612 $= 612 +$		
			3 O=O bonds at 498 $= \underline{1494}$		
			total for bonds broken 3758 kJ	2	
			You would lose a mark for each error, up to 2 marks.		
			Bonds made:		
			4 C=O bonds at 805 $= 3220$		
			4 H—O bonds at 464 $= \underline{1856}$		
			total for bonds made $= 5076$ kJ	2	
			The difference between bonds broken and bonds made is 1318 kJ.	1	
		ii	The reaction is exothermic as energy is released.	1	
	b		*Any three from:*		
			• increase the pressure (if a gas is involved)		
			• increase the temperature		
			• increase the concentration		
			• lower the activation energy / use a catalyst.	3	**9 marks**
3	a		M_r of sodium chloride is 58	1	
			116 g represents two moles	1	
			1 mole of chlorine is released ($2NaCl \rightarrow 2Na + Cl_2$)	1	
			1 mole occupies 24 litres at room temperature and pressure.	1	
	b		Calcium Chlorine		
			40 35 atomic mass	1	
			20 35 mass reacting	1	
			0.5 1 moles reacting		
			1 2 converted to whole numbers	1	
			The formula is $CaCl_2$.	1	**8 marks**

Question			Answer	Marks	Total
4	a		*Any four of:* barley, maize grits, water, hops, liquid sugar.	2	
	b		The enzyme catalyses the reaction.	1	
	c		Carbon dioxide.	1	
	d	i	Exothermic.	1	
		ii	Above a certain temperature enzymes denature (are destroyed).	1	
	e		Higher temperatures give particles more energy	1	
			so they move around faster and more likely to hit each other	1	
			and when they do they hit with more energy.	1	**9 marks**

Total for test: 39 marks

Structures and bonding

Question			Answer	Marks	Total
1	a	i	39	1	
		ii	19	1	
		iii	20	1	
	b		*1 mark each for showing:*		
			2 electrons in inner shell	1	
			8 electrons in next shell and	1	
			1 electron in outer shell.	1	
	c	i	Lithium as 2,1 (electronic structure)	1	
			chlorine as 2, 8, 7 (electronic structure)	1	
			outer electron of lithium joins outer shell of chlorine.	1	
		ii	Ionic.	1	
		iii	An ion is an atom	1	
			with a charge.	1	
			It loses	1	
			one electron.	1	**14 marks**
2	a		Atoms	1	
			held together	1	
			by bonds.	1	
	b		1N 3H $H \overset{\times\times}{\underset{\times\bullet}{\times N \times}} H$ $\underset{H}{}$ $\overset{\times}{\times}$ [1] $3(\overset{\times}{\bullet})$ [1] correct arrangement [1]	3	
	c		The bonds holding them together	1	
			are weaker/more easily broken.	1	**8 marks**
3	a	i	$2K + 2H_2O \rightarrow 2KOH + H_2$	1	
		ii	Outer electron is closer to nucleus	1	
			so is less easily lost	1	
			as greater attraction to nucleus.	1	
	b		Chlorine more reactive	1	
			so displaces the iodine.	1	**6 marks**

Question			Answer	Marks	Total
4	**a**		So that the ions are free to move.	1 1	
	b		Sodium ions are attracted each gains an electron to become a sodium atom.	1 1 1	
	c	**i**	*Any two from*: • kill bacteria (water/swimming pools) • bleach • disinfectant • production of polymers (for example, PVC).	 2	
		ii	Bleaches damp litmus paper.	1 1 1	**10 marks**
5	**a**	**i**	1 atom of hydrogen 1 atom of chlorine they share outer electrons.	1 1 1	
		ii	1 proton 0 neutrons 1 electron.	1 1 1	
	b	**i**	2 atoms bonded together to form the molecule (for example, O_2).	1	
		ii	*Marks for showing in the diagram*: 2 oxygen atoms each with 6 electrons in outer shell they each share 2 electrons with the other atom.	 1 1 1	
	c		*Any four points from*: • each carbon atom • is covalently bonded • to four others • the structure is rigid • it is a giant structure.	 4	**14 marks**

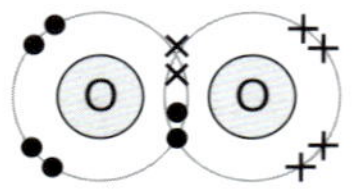

Total for test: 52 marks

Energy

Question	Answer	Marks	Total
1	1 solar 2 nuclear 3 wind 4 coal	1 1 1 1	4
2	1 joule 2 metre 3 newton 4 watt	1 1 1 1	4
3	1 radiation 2 waves 3 vacuum 4 conduction	1 1 1 1	4
4	B and E	2	2
5	A and D	2	2

Question	Answer		Marks	Total
6	1.	B	1	
	2.	C	1	
	3.	B	1	
	4.	A	1	4
7	1.	D	1	
	2.	A	1	
	3.	C	1	
	4.	D	1	4
8	1.	B	1	
	2.	C	1	
	3.	A	1	
	4.	D	1	4

Total for test: 28 marks

Electricity

Question	Answer	Marks	Total
1	1 diode 2 fuse 3 resistor 4 thermistor	1 1 1 1	4
2	1 diode 2 LDR 3 thermistor 4 resistor	1 1 1 1	4
3	1 battery 2 force field 3 split ring 4 current	1 1 1 1	4
4	B and D	2	2
5	A and C	2	2

Question	Answer		Marks	Total
6	1.	C	1	
	2.	B	1	
	3.	D	1	
	4.	B	1	4
7	1.	D	1	
	2.	B	1	
	3.	A	1	
	4.	D	1	4
8	1.	C	1	
	2.	C	1	
	3.	A	1	
	4.	D	1	4

Total for test: 28 marks

Forces

Question			Answer	Marks	Total
1	a		average speed $= \dfrac{\text{distance (m)}}{\text{time (s)}}$	1	
			$= \dfrac{600}{240}$		
			$= 2.5 \, \text{m/s}$	1	
	b		weight $=$ mass $\times$ gravitational field strength		
			$= 50 \times 10$		
			$= 500 \, \text{N}$	1	
			work done $=$ force applied $\times$ distance moved in direction of the force	1	
			$= 500 \times 12$		
			$= 6000$	1	
			N	1	
			Note: it is common in the higher level questions to have to work out the answer to one question and use this answer to solve a second problem.		**6 marks**
2	a	i	A combination of: high speed	1	
			and gravity.	1	
		ii	It will take longer.	1	
	b	i	Geostationary.	1	
		ii	So that they are in contact with same part of the Earth's surface the whole time.	1	
	c	i	Polar orbit.	1	
		ii	So that they can see all of the Earth's surface over a period of time	1	**7 marks**
3	a		29 000 N	1	
	b	i	The magnitude of force A begins to decrease.	1	
		ii	Force B remains the same. However, due to the water running out the mass of the car decreases and therefore the magnitude of force A. Force A and force B are now unbalanced and car begins to move up the hill.	1	
	c		Force A and force B are equal	1	
	d		One newton is the force needed to give a mass of 1 kg an acceleration of 1 m/s^2	2	**6 marks**

Total for test: 19 marks

Waves and radiation

Question			Answer	Marks	Total
1	a		Transverse (*but mark only given if explanation given*)	1	
			because disturbances	1	
			at right angles to direction of travel.	1	
	b	i	wave speed = frequency × wavelength	1	
			therefore: wavelength = $\dfrac{\text{wave speed}}{\text{frequency}}$	1	
			$= \dfrac{0.3}{2}$		
			$= 0.15$	1	
			m(etres)	1	
		ii		1	
	c			1	
		ii	Change in speed	1	
			as it crosses the boundary.	1	**11 marks**
2	a	i	Alpha and beta.	2	
		ii	Alpha and gamma.	2	
	b	i	*Any three points from*:		
			• inside the body		
			• they can't pass through skin		
			• strongly absorbed by cells		
			• ionising.	3	
		ii	Two neutrons	1	
			two protons	1	
			a helium nucleus.	1	
	c		*Any two from*:		
			• X-rays for broken bones		
			• killing cancer cells		
			• sterilising equipment.	2	
	d	i	100 s	1	
		ii	300 s	1	
			3 half-lives	1	**15 marks**
3	a		Seismographs.	1	
	b	i	Curves because it refracts	1	
			gentle curve as density changing gradually	1	
			won't pass through solid	1	
			so changes direction abruptly at point X.	1	
		ii	Will pass through solids	1	
			changes abruptly at points Y and Z as density changes abruptly.	1	
		iii	Wave A is an S wave	1	
			wave B is a P wave.	1	**9 marks**

Question			Answer	Marks	Total
4	a		Refracts back towards normal	1	
			leaves block at 45 degrees.	1	
			In second diagram ray passes straight through, no change in direction.	1	
	b		Different colours have different wavelengths	1	
			so they refract to different extents.	1	
	c	i	Seeing	1	
			into people's bodies/gut/blood vessels.	1	
		ii	Light down an optical fibre	1	
			totally internally reflected	1	
			angle between light and normal greater than critical angle	1	
			light rays emerge at the end.	1	
	d	i	Radiation that can pass through space/a vacuum	1	
			no particles involved.	1	
		ii	*1 mark deducted for each mistake (maximum loss of 3 marks):*		
			1 gamma rays		
			2 UV rays		
			3 light rays		
			4 microwaves.	3	
			1 mark deducted for each mistake (maximum loss of 3 marks):		
			1 X-rays		
			2 light rays		
			3 infra red rays		
			4 radio waves.	3	**19 marks**
5	a	i	33% ± 1%	1	
		ii	100 days (5 half-lives).	1	
	b		Work out the proportion of the radioactive substance compared to the substance it decays to.	1	
			Find out the half-life of the radioactive substance.	1	
			Work out how many half-lives have passed and multiply this figure by the number of years for one half-life.	1	
	c		Sterilise food	1	
			sterilise surgical instruments	1	
			kill cancer cells.	1	
	d		*Any three points from:*		
			• waves strongly absorbed		
			• by water		
			• causes increased vibration of particles		
			• the friction caused results in heat.	3	**11 marks**

Total for test: 65 marks

Answers to end of spread questions

These notes accompany the questions that are to be found at the end of each double-page spread. They are not mark schemes as these questions are not the same as those you will find in your final examination. Where candidates have common misconceptions, these are added to the notes.

Humans as organisms

PAGE 3

1

Enzyme	Where made	What does it do?
carbohydrase	salivary gland pancreas small intestine	digests starch to sugars
protease	stomach pancreas small intestine	digests protein to amino acids
lipase	pancreas small intestine	digests fats to fatty acids and glycerol

2 Acidic conditions.

3 Increases the surface area for enzymes to work on. *Pupils frequently do not know this.*

PAGE 5

1 Glucose: in blood from small intestine from food you eat. *In a later section you will find that some may be converted to glycogen in the liver to be stored if there is already too much sugar in the blood.*
Oxygen: absorbed into blood through alveoli, picked up by haemoglobin and transported to respiring cells in body where it is released. *This is dealt with in detail on the next spread.*

2 It is carried in capillaries away from the cells. Eventually the capillaries form veins. It is transported through the heart and on to the lungs where it diffuses through the alveoli and is breathed out.

3 There is a greater surface area for the gas to diffuse through. This prevents any build up (rather like preventing a traffic jam). *You will find this idea of surface area very important in biology.*

4 Diffusion is the movement of particles from an area of higher concentration to an area of lower concentration. There is a greater concentration of oxygen in the lungs than in the blood returning from the body so oxygen diffuses into the blood. The exact opposite is true for carbon dioxide.

5 When we breathe out the ribs move down and in, the diaphragm moves up, this causes an increase in pressure on the air in the lungs – so we breathe out.

6 To break down the lactic acid that has built up.

PAGE 7

1 Plasma transports a great many things. Those you need to know are: carbon dioxide, digested food and urea.

2 Veins have thinner walls with less muscle and elastic tissue. They also have valves to prevent backflow of blood. *Remember there are also valves in the heart to prevent backflow of blood.*

3 There are many substances exchanged. Those you need to know are: oxygen, carbon dioxide and digested food.

4 White cells help defend the body against microorganisms (they ingest or eat them). Red cells transport oxygen (in the haemoglobin as oxy-haemoglobin). Platelets help form scabs over cuts.

5 The red cell passes into the ventricle then the main artery. It then passes into the capillaries that form the blood supply to an organ (for example, the liver). It will then pass into a vein leading away from the organ. It will eventually find its way into the main vein taking blood back to the right atrium of the heart.

PAGE 9

1 Viruses have a protein coat surrounding a few genes. There is no cell membrane or nucleus.

2 Toxins are poisons (often produced by invading microorganisms). White cells produce anti-toxins to neutralise them.

3 White cells will attack the microorganisms. White cells may produce antibodies and antitoxins to help destroy particular microorganisms.

4 By having a complete skin (that is, a skin without any cuts in it). By having the air passages covered in a sticky mucus that helps trap any microorganisms being breathed in. Also the stomach is acidic.

5 People in much closer contact allow microorganisms to transfer from one person to another either by touch or in droplets (for example, sneezing).

Maintenance of life

PAGE 13

1 Your spider diagram should include: cell wall, chlorophyll (chloroplasts) and vacuole.

2 Too cold and less light; enzymes controlling photosynthesis only working very slowly.

3 Diffuses in from air, through stomata, then diffuses through large air spaces to all cells, it then diffuses through the cell walls.
   Note: a question like this could well be worth 4 marks in an exam. Make sure you write in the necessary detail.

4 Starch for storage, cellulose for cell walls, combined with other nutrients to produce proteins for growth.

5 It would have poorly formed roots and the younger leaves would have a purple colour.

6 $\text{carbon dioxide} + \text{water} \xrightarrow[\text{chlorophyll}]{\text{light}} \text{glucose} + \text{oxygen}$

PAGE 15

1 Large surface area.

2 Movement of water from an area where there is a higher concentration of water molecules to one where the concentration is lower.

3 Your diagram should include: to help new cuttings grow roots, to help ripen fruit, and as weedkillers.

PAGE 17

1 The hot kettle is the stimulus, sensory nerve endings in the fingers are triggered, a message passes along the sensory nerve to the spinal chord. A relay nerve is triggered and this passes the message on to the correct motor nerve. This nerve takes the message to an effector – in this case a muscle that contracts pulling your hand away from the kettle.

2 The impulse is an electrical message sent through the nerves. Then chemicals are released across the synapses.

3 When watching the television the lens was its natural shape (quite thick). This is necessary to bend light rays, which are diverging quickly, to a focus. When looking at your friend the rays of light are not diverging quickly so do not need to be bent as much. The ciliary muscles relax, ligaments attached to the lens pull on the lens, the lens becomes thinner.

PAGE 19

1 You are respiring quickly to release energy. Some energy is released as heat so you need to cool down. Blood vessels near the skin's surface dilate to allow more blood to flow near the surface. The blood radiates heat. The skin looks red.

2 You have lost a lot of water in sweating. The blood contains less water – it is concentrated. The pituitary gland releases ADH. The kidney tubule walls become more permeable and reabsorb more water. The urine is therefore more concentrated.

3 Liver and brain.

4 The circulatory system.

5 It slows down reactions.

Environment

PAGE 23

1 The kestrel is the predator and the mice are prey.

2 The kestrel population would rise as there would be more food to feed their young. The mouse population would, as a result, decrease.

3 Your diagram should refer to: the amount of food available, the number of predators, disease, competition with other animals for the food available.

4 Your food web should show the two producers – seeds and berries. Birds are eating the seeds and berries, mice are eating the seeds only. The mice and birds are being eaten by the kestrels.

PAGE 25

1 Because a pyramid of numbers does not take account of the fact that some organisms are much larger than others (for example, a tree and a caterpillar).

2 There are many ways including: excretion, movement, radiated as heat, all of the food is not digested in the first place.

3 If the materials that are removed from the environment are not replaced then they would eventually run out and life would stop.

PAGE 27

1 Photosynthesising, respiring, decomposing, respiring.

2 Carbohydrates, fats and proteins.

3 The dead bodies are decomposed by bacteria, the protein is broken down into ammonium compounds, the ammonium compounds are converted to nitrates by nitrifying bacteria.

PAGE 29

1 Sulphur dioxide given off, dissolves in rain, this makes the rain acidic as it falls on the lake. The lake water becomes acidic. Enzymes in organisms are very pH dependant. If the enzymes denature because of the acidity the organism dies. *Note: this last point on enzymes is frequently forgotten but is the most important point.*

2 The plants grow quickly, the surface of the pond will quickly become covered by plants. Many plants die. They may fall to the bottom where bacteria will decompose them. Bacteria use up oxygen in this decomposition as they are respiring. There is too little oxygen left for other animals. The process is called eutrophication.

3 You should mention: fewer trees to take it up, alongside this more is being produced by combustion (for example, cars, power stations, burning trees).

4 *This question asks for your own opinions. As long as they are well informed and argued you will be awarded marks.*

Inheritance and selection

PAGE 33

1 Environmental and genetic.

2 A copy of each chromosome is made so that there are now four of each type of chromosome in the cell. The cell divides twice so that each new cell has only one chromosome from each original pair.

3 Because they have exactly the same genetic make up.

4 41 chromosomes, one from each original pair.

PAGE 35

1 Bacteria producing insulin. *Note: if you know a well known example try to use it, some examiners may not have heard of more unusual ones.*

2 The programme only used a certain type of the species – the most attractive ones! The gene pool of the species was therefore reduced (there was less variety of genes present in the population). When disease struck, the gene that helped the animals fight off the disease was no longer present in the population.

3 Taking part of an organism (for example, a cutting or a cell) and growing a new member of the species from it. The cell division is mitosis.

4 Women who were unable to produce eggs can now produce eggs and now have a chance of mothering their own children. However, this treatment can result in too many eggs being produced and an increased chance of multiple births. Multiple births are more hazardous for both the babies and the mother.

PAGE 37

1 One parent is SS the other is Ss. The possible combinations of the genes in the offspring are SS SS Ss or Ss. There is therefore a 50% chance of a child being a carrier (Ss).

2 If the parents do not have the disorder the parents must both be hh as the allele that results in the disorder is dominant (H). There is no chance of any of their children having the disorder.

1 They have become trapped in the amber where there is no oxygen present. Bacteria cannot decompose them as they cannot respire due to the lack of oxygen. *Note: it must be apparent to you that a number of examination answers rely on the fact that bacteria respire and use up oxygen when they decompose dead organisms.*

2 Any three of: X-rays, UV light, radiation, some chemicals.

3 Pale moths are camouflaged against predators where tree trunks are grey. They therefore survive to breed and dark ones are eaten. The opposite applies in industrial areas.

4 Your diagram should include: environmental change, predators wipe them out, disease wipes them out, a new species evolves that competes successfully with the species.

5 Some bacteria are resistant to antibiotics. The antibiotics kill all non-resistant bacteria. The resistant bacteria, without competition from non-resistant bacteria, can multiply making infection by resistant bacteria more and more likely.

Metals

PAGE 43

1 *Any two from*: Lithium (Li), Sodium (Na). Potassium (K), Rubidium (Rb), Caesium (Cs), Francium (Fr).

2 Groups.

3 Zinc would displace the copper. That is copper would precipitate out and zinc chloride solution would form.

4 *The spider diagram should include*: good conductors of heat, good conductors of electricity, can be easily bent or hammered into different shapes.

5 Mercury is a liquid at room termperature.

PAGE 45

1 To react with impurities and form molten slag.

2 It is less reactive than aluminium so nothing would happen.

3 It is melted so that electricity will be conducted. It is dissolved in molten cryolite to reduce its melting point and save the manufacturer money. *Note: if there is an economic point to make in the answer to a question then it is always advisable to mention it.*

4 Magnesium.

PAGE 47

1 A reaction where one reactant is reduced whilst another reactant is oxidised.

2 Wet and salty conditions.

3 A reaction where hydrogen ions are reacted with hydroxide ions.

4 potassium chloride   potassium sulphate
calcium chloride   calcium sulphate

5 potassium + hydrochloric → potassium + water
hydroxide   acid   chloride
or KOH + HCl → KCl + H_2O

Earth materials

PAGE 51

1 The crust floats on the layer beneath it. Therefore, this layer must be denser than the crust.

2 Metamorphic rocks are formed from other rocks that are put under great pressure and heat at the same time. This is most likely to occur where mountains are forming.

PAGE 53

1 Their shapes seem to fit together and they seem to have similar rocks and fossils.

2 Tectonic plates sliding past each other. Movements of the plates cause earthquakes.

3 The magnetic stripes are basically iron rich magma. The iron lines up in the direction of the Earth's magnetic field. This field changes. There is therefore an indication of when the magma erupted showing that the sea floor is spreading.

PAGE 55

1 Water is added to quicklime (calcium oxide).

2 Oil is a mixture.

3 Short-chain hydrocarbons burn easily, evaporate quite quickly and are generally gases or liquids – no use for roads! Long-chain hydrocarbons are thick (very viscous) and do not burn easily – no use for fuels!

PAGE 57

1 One of the bonds in the carbon–carbon double bond can break leaving the two carbon atoms free to react with another element.

2 Not all long-chain hydrocarbons can be used. There may be too many of them. They can be broken ('cracked') into short-chain hydrocarbons that may be useful as fuels, etc. Essentially they are 'cracked' so that oil companies can make more money! Alkenes also result, which can be used to make plastics.

3 They may give off chemicals that are harmful to the environment.

PAGE 59

1 Ammonia, methane, carbon dioxide, water vapour.

2 Partly due to the reaction between ammonia and oxygen and partly due to organisms evolving that subsequently died and decomposed releasing nitrogen. Denitrifying bacteria are involved in this nitrogen release.

3 Less carbon dioxide as it became locked up in sedimentary rocks and fossil fuels as well as being used by plants in photosynthesis. Less ammonia and methane because they reacted with oxygen (given off by plants). More oxygen due to photosynthesising plants. The oxygen also helped develop an ozone layer protecting us from the Sun's radiation (UV rays). *Note: these changes in the atmosphere questions are nearly always poorly answered, even by the best of candidates.*

4 Carbon dioxide and water vapour.

Patterns of chemical change

PAGE 63

1 *Any three of:* increase temperature – particles bump into each other more often with more energy; increase concentration – particles bump into each other more often; increase pressure (gases only) – particles bump into each other more often; increase surface area of reactants – particles bump into each other more often; use a catalyst – lowers the amount of 'activation' energy required.

2 Chemicals that speed up reactions – they are used to lower costs.

3 Make more product or make more profit.

PAGE 65

1 A reaction that releases heat.

2 One atom of nitrogen reacts with two atoms of oxygen, you must 'add' energy to make them react, the product is nitrogen dioxide and it is at a higher energy level than the reactants. Therefore the reaction is endothermic.

3 Endothermic.

PAGE 67

1 A reaction that, depending on the conditions, will go either way.

3 It would be expensive to create temperatures of 350 °C and equally expensive to create reaction vessels capable of withstanding pressures of 400 atmospheres.

PAGE 69

1 $Ca = 40$
$2 \times H = 2$
$2 \times O = 32$
Answer $= 74$

2 $1 \times Ca = 40$
$1 \times C = 12$
$3 \times 16 = 48$ Total $= 100$
of which oxygen $= 48$
or 48%

Structures and bonding

PAGE 73

1 2, 8, 7.

2 Four.

3 Magnesium 2, 8, 2; silicon 2, 8, 4; argon 2, 8, 8; oxygen 2, 8, 6.

PAGE 75

1 Your diagram of calcium should have 2 electrons in the first and fourth shells with eight electrons in the second and third shells.

2 Calcium needs to lose two electrons, chlorine can gain only one electron. Therefore calcium needs two chlorine atoms to react with. The formula of calcium chloride must be $CaCl_2$.

3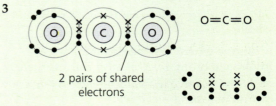

2 pairs of shared electrons

PAGE 77

1 The bonds between molecules are generally weak and easily broken.

2 Each carbon atom is covalently bonded to four other carbon atoms. The structure is a giant structure that is rigid owing to the strong bonds between the atoms.

3 $2H_2O_2 \rightarrow 2H_2O + O_2$

PAGE 79

1 The one outer electron in potassium is at a higher energy level than that of the outer electron in sodium, as it is further from the nucleus. The electron is therefore more easily 'lost'.

2 When they react with water an alkaline solution is left (for example, sodium reacts with water to produce sodium hydroxide with hydrogen gas evolving).

3 They have a complete outer shell of electrons.

4 Xenon is present simply as single atoms. In chlorine two atoms bond together, covalently, to form a molecule of the gas (hence diatomic).

PAGE 81

1 Your diagram should include: chlorine used for killing bacteria, it is also used in disinfectants, bleaches and to produce plastics (for example, PVC or polyvinyl chloride); hydrogen is used in the production of ammonia and margarine; sodium hydroxide is used in the production of soap, paper and ceramics.

2 Chloride ions are attracted, they lose electrons to become atoms, pairs covalently bond together to form chlorine gas molecules that evolve. *Note: in an examination a question like this could be worth 4 marks – it would be insufficient to state simply that chlorine gas evolves.*

3 They only need to gain one electron as they are only one electron 'short' in the outer shell.

4 Chlorine would displace bromine from hydrogen bromide. *Remember that reactivity decreases as you go down the group – the opposite to the alkali metals in Group 1.*

Energy

PAGE 85

1 Free electrons can transfer heat energy to cooler parts of the bar.

2 Radiation.

3 The air above the radiator warms up. It becomes less dense. The air rises. It spreads across the ceiling and cools a little. It becomes denser and so falls in other parts of the room. It is still quite warm and therefore the person feels the warmer air. Some heat will also be radiated from the radiator.

4 Air between the bricks is still likely to warm slightly – the insulation prevents convection of this air. Such convection would draw cooler air into the bottom of the wall.

PAGE 87

1 $\dfrac{1500\,(J)}{60\,(s)} = 25\,W$

2 $30\,000 \times (90 \times 60) = 162\,000\,000\,J$

3 $378 \times £0.45 = £17.01$

PAGE 89

1 Hair drier as movement (the fan) and heat; toaster as heat; television as sound and light; vacuum cleaner as movement.

2 Double glazing $\dfrac{2000}{80} = 25$ years

Draught excluders $\dfrac{30}{40} = 0.75$ years

Cavity wall insulation $\dfrac{1000}{30} = 33\frac{1}{3}$ years

Extra roof insulation $\dfrac{300}{100} = 3$ years

At 0.75 years to repay the cost of installation, draught excluders are the best value for money.

3 Nuclear power stations are non-polluting. However, the radioactive waste they produce must be disposed of safely. Some of it can still be dangerous even after many thousands of years.
Fossil fuel power stations do not produce radioactive waste. However, they do pollute the atmosphere with carbon dioxide (a Greenhouse Gas) and sulphur dioxide, which causes acid rain.

PAGE 91

1   Examples might include:

Energy source	Advantage	Disadvantage
coal	fairly cheap	will eventually run out
hydroelectric	renewable	only useful in certain areas
nuclear	much energy from a small amount of fuel	non-renewable
wind turbine	renewable	spoils the landscape
tidal	renewable	expensive to set up

2   Hydroelectric, wind turbine, tidal.

3   Hilltops as they are exposed to the wind, coastal areas as there is more likelihood of wind, off-shore as this is less unsightly.

Electricity

PAGE 95

1   You can show how power can be calculated using this series of equations:

$$\text{power (watts)} = \frac{\text{energy transferred (joules)}}{\text{time (seconds)}}$$

$$\underset{\text{(joules)}}{\text{energy transferred}} = \underset{\text{(volts)}}{\text{potential difference}} \times \underset{\text{(coulombs)}}{\text{charge}}$$

$$\text{charge (coulombs)} = \text{current (amps)} \times \text{time}$$

$$\text{power (watts)} = \frac{\text{potential difference} \times \text{current} \times \cancel{\text{time}}}{\cancel{\text{time}}}$$

$$\underset{\text{(watts)}}{\text{power}} = \underset{\text{(volts)}}{\text{potential difference}} \times \underset{\text{(amps)}}{\text{current}}$$

2   The electricity passes through a filament that offers resistance. As well as the filament becoming hot some energy is emitted as light.

PAGE 97

1   In the first graph: the current is directly proportional to the voltage (this means it increases at the same rate). If you reverse the voltage you reverse the current.
In the second graph: at first the current increases rapidly as you increase the voltage, however as you further increase the voltage the current increases more and more slowly. If you reverse the voltage you reverse the current.

In the third graph: the current is directly proportional to the voltage. However if you reverse the voltage you get very little current flowing at all. This component offers great resistance to current flowing in the 'wrong' direction.

2   Exposure to light causes the static charge to leak away. This means that only areas not exposed to the light will attract the dark powder.

PAGE 99

1   The current is continually changing direction.

2   They can be reset quickly and work more quickly than a fuse.

PAGE 101

1   The secondary coil has 50 times as many turns as the primary coil. The voltage induced will, therefore, be 50 times greater than the input voltage. $50 \times 200 = 10\,000$ V.

2   You want the output voltage to be $\frac{1}{25}$ of the input voltage $\frac{5000}{200}$. The ratio of primary coils to secondary coils is therefore 25:1.

Forces

PAGE 105

1   Average velocity = distance/time
$$= \frac{60}{4} = 15 \text{ m/s}$$
Acceleration = change in velocity/time
$$= \frac{(60 - 0)}{4} = \frac{60}{4} = 15 \text{ m/s}^2$$

2   Your graph should have these features:

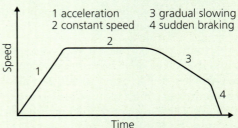

1 acceleration   3 gradual slowing
2 constant speed 4 sudden braking

3   Velocity is speed in a straight line (velocity is a vector).

PAGE 107

1   For example, if your mass is 57 kg then your weight is 57×10 N or 570 N.

2   The downward force due to the weight of the boat (due to gravity) is balanced by the upward force of the water.

3 There is a backward force exerted by the car engine. There is a force resisting this caused by both air resistance and the friction of the tyres on the ground. The forces are unbalanced so the car moves backwards.

4 Kinetic energy = $\frac{1}{2}mv^2$
Therefore $(\frac{1}{2} \times 100) \times 30^2$.
This equals 50×900 or $45\,000$ J or 45 kJ.

PAGE 109

1 Force = mass × acceleration.
Therefore force = $1000 \times 6 = 6000$ N. *Note: the weight of the car was $10\,000$ N therefore its mass is 1000 kg.*

2 *Possible answers include:* snow, ice, rain or oil on the road.

3 The force of gravity causes the stone to accelerate as it falls. At a certain speed the pressure of the air prevents the stone falling any faster. The forces are now balanced and the stone falls at steady speed. This steady speed is known as the terminal velocity. *Note: never answer this question just by stating 'terminal velocity'. The question asks what has happened not what is it called.*

PAGE 111

1 The further the planet is from the Sun the longer it takes to complete an orbit of the Sun.

2 Placed in orbit high above the equator, at the same speed as the Earth is spinning.

3 So that the Earth spins below; the whole of the Earth can be scanned in a day.

4 In the stable period the star stays the same size as the forces of attraction (between all of the particles, due to gravity) and repulsion (due to the very high temperatures) are balanced. The forces of repulsion will start to 'win' and the star will become a red giant. These forces then begin to decrease and so the force of gravity becomes the larger force. The star contracts to become a white dwarf. If the star was large enough and contraction takes place quickly then it may explode and become a supernova. A very dense neutron star remains. *Note: a question about this may be worth about 5 marks – do not waffle make sure that you write down five correct facts in the right order.*

PAGE 113

1 As galaxies are moving apart quickly the wavelength of light is increasing. As it increases red light moves into the far red part of the spectrum. This is known as the 'red shift'.

2 As galaxies move away light is shifted to the red end of the spectrum.

3 A black hole is a neutron star that is so dense that nothing, not even light, can escape from its gravitational field.

4 Without photosynthesising life there would be no oxygen in the Earth's atmosphere. If oxygen were in the atmosphere of another planet this might be an indication of life.

Waves and radiation

PAGE 117

1 As the light passes from one substance into a substance of a different density it changes speed. This change of speed results in the light bending. This is known as refraction.

2

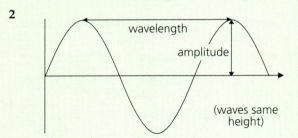

wavelength

amplitude

(waves same height)

PAGE 119

1 A light is shone down the endoscope. The light totally internally reflects so emerges only at the end of the endoscope. It internally reflects because the angle at which the light 'hits' the side of the endoscope is greater than the critical angle.

2 As the water enters the harbour entrance the waves spread out from the edges and cause the boat to 'bob'. This is known as diffraction.

3 They have a higher quality. Even if the pulses weaken they still can be recognised as 'on' or 'off'.

PAGE 121

1 They are checking for structural defects (for example, cracks).

2 P waves travel through solids and liquids. S waves only pass through liquids. They both refract as they pass into substances of a different density. *(Note: liquids will also change in density.)* If you know the point of the Earth the shock wave starts from and where it can be detected as it is felt at a different point of the Earth's surface, then you can work out the densities of the substances it has passed through to result in the refraction the wave has experienced.

PAGE 123

1 X-rays (shortest), UV, microwave, radio waves (longest).

2 *Any two of:* electric grills, toasters, heaters, optical fibres and video remote controls.

3 Long waves can be 'bounced off' off the ionsphere and can therefore be transmitted around the Earth despite its curvature.

PAGE 125

1 It may cause them to heat up and therefore be damaged or killed.

2 Beta and gamma radiation will pass through very thick paper.

3 Uranium loses an alpha particle (two protons and two electrons). Thorium loses a beta particle (and one proton becomes a neutron).

PAGE 127

1 200 years (two half-lives).

2 Uranium has 92 protons and 92 electrons (so as an atom is electrically neutral). It has 146 neutrons.

3 $\frac{1}{4}$

Index

AQA

MODULAR

science

Nigel English

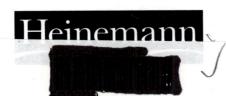

Heinemann

Heinemann Educational Publishers
Halley Court, Jordan Hill, Oxford, OX2 8EJ
a division of Reed Educational & Professional Publishing Ltd

Heinemann is a registered trademark of Reed Educational & Professional
Publishing Ltd.

OXFORD   MELBOURNE   AUCKLAND   JOHANNESBURG
BLANTYRE   GABORNE   IBADAN   PORTSMOUTH (NH)   CHICAGO

First published 1997

ISBN 0 453 10026 2

04 03 02
10 9 8 7 6 5 4 3 2 1

Edited by Sarah Ware and Allan Masson

Typeset and illustrated by Tech Set Ltd

Printed and bound in Italy by Printer Trento S.r.l

Acknowledgements
Cover photo by Digitalvision

Photos on pp 1, 41 and 83 by PhotoDisk